Steck-Vaughn

BOOK 2

World Geography and You

Vivian Bernstein

STECK-VAUGHN
C O M P A N Y
A Subsidiary of National Education Corporation

About the Author

Vivian Bernstein has been a teacher in the New York City Public School System for a number of years. She received her Master of Arts degree from New York University. Bernstein is active with professional organizations in social studies, education, and reading. She is the author of *America's Story*, *World History and You*, and *Health and You*.

Acknowledgments

Cover Photography: Rick Patrick
Cover Photographs: © Comstock Inc.

Unit 1: 6-7 Picturesque Palestine; 7 © FourByFive/Superstock; 8 © IFA/UNIPHOTO; 10 © Dennis Degnan/UNIPHOTO; 11 © Paolo Koch/Photo Researchers; 12 © Ed Drews/Photo Researchers; 16 © W. Shattil & B. Rozinski/Tom Stack Associates; 18 © Owen Franken/Stock, Boston; 19 Courtesy Egyptian State Tourist Administration; 20 © Gerhardt Liebmann/Photo Researchers; 24 © Hubertus Kanus/Photo Researchers; p. 26 © Ellan Young/Photo Researchers; 27 UPI/Bettmann Newsphotos; 30 © Paolo Koch/Photo Researchers; 32 © Owen Franken/Stock, Boston; 33 © Louis Goldman/Photo Researchers; 34 © Bernard Wolff/Photo Researchers; 37 © Tim Carlson/Stock, Boston; 38 © Owen Franken/Stock; Boston; 39 © Paolo Koch/Photo Researchers; 40 AP/Wide World; 41 AP/Wide World; 44 © Alon Reininger/Woodfin Camp Associates; 45 © Comstock, Inc.;

Unit 2: 46-47 Historical Pictures Service, Chicago; 47 © Paul Conklin/UNIPHOTO; 48 © Ira Kirschenbaum/Stock, Boston; 50 © Robert Caputo/Stock, Boston; 51 © Charles G. Summers/Tom Stack Associates; 53 © Don Fawcett/Tom Stack Associates; 56 © Abbas/Magnum; 59 © Owen Franken/Stock, Boston; 60 © Tom Cheek/Stock, Boston; 64 © John Moss/Photo Researchers; 65 © Blair Seitz/Photo Researchers; 66 © Farrell Grehan/Photo Researchers; 70 AP/Wide World; 73 © Pat Lanza Field/Bruce Coleman, Inc.; 74 Courtesy South African Tourist Corp.; 77 © Marc & Evelyne Bernheim/Woodfin Camp Associates; 78 © Owen Franken/Stock, Boston; 79 © Sven-Olof Lindblad/Photo Researchers; 81 © Owen Franken/Stock, Boston; 84 © Comstock, Inc.;

Unit 3: 86-87 Historical Pictures Service, Chicago; 87 © Comstock, Inc.; 88 © Stuart Cohen/Stock, Boston; 90 © George Bellerose/Stock, Boston; 91 © H. Armstrong Roberts; 92 © Robert Frerck/Odyssey Productions; 93 © B. Barbey/Magnum; 96 © Jean-Claude Lejeune/Stock, Boston; 99 © Cary S. Wolinsky/Stock, Boston; 100 © Jean-Claude Lejeune/Stock, Boston; 104 © B. Barbey/Magnum; 105 © Dennis Stock/Magnum; 106 © Robert Frerck/Odyssey Productions; 107 © Manfred Gottschalk/Tom Stack Associates; 110 © Michael K. Nichols/Magnum; 112 © Paolo Koch/Photo Researchers; 113 © Owen Franken/Stock, Boston; 114 © Michael K. Nichols/Magnum; 118 © Haruhart Prapahya/Gamma-Liaison, p. 119 © Abbas/Magnum; 120 © Michael K. Nichols/Magnum; 121 AP/Wide World; 125 © Art Wolfe/The Image Bank;

Unit 4: 126-127 Granger Collection; 127 © Comstock, Inc.; 128 © Mickey Gibson/Tom Stack Associates; 130 © Dallas & John Heaton/Stock, Boston; 131 © Rick Smolan/Stock, Boston; 132 © Xinhun/Gamma-Liaison; 136 © Manfred Gottschalk/Tom Stack Associates; 139 © Ira Kirschenbaum/Stock, Boston; 140 AP/Wide World; 144 © H. Armstrong Roberts; 145 © Julie Houck/Stock, Boston; 147 © J.R. Holland/Stock, Boston; 150 © Robert Frerck/Odyssey Productions; 153 © Frederick Ayer/Photo Researchers; 154 © Robert Frerck/Odyssey Productions; 157 © Shi Guanda/Xinhua News Agency; 158 © Xinhua News Agency; 159 © Sheryl S. McNee/Tom Stack Associates; 161 © Charles Gupton/Stock, Boston; 165 © Kaku Kuritz/Gamma-Liaison.

Consultants:

Alan L. Backler, Ph.D.: Dr. Backler has written several geography texts and has produced media materials in the field of geography.

Ann Grabhorn-Friday, M.Ed.: Ms. Grabhorn-Friday teaches geography at both the high school and community college level in Austin, TX.

Staff Credits:

Supervising Editor: Diane Sharpe
Project Editor: Athena O. Kildegaard
Photo Editor: Margie Matejcik

Art Director: Scott Huber
Electronic Production: Alan Klemp

ISBN 0-8114-7976-5

Table of Contents

To the Reader

In Book One of *World Geography and You*, you read about North and South America, Europe, and Russia and its neighbors. You began learning about geography. Geography is the study of Earth. You learned that some nations are very modern, while others are not at all modern. You read about people who live like you do, and people who live very different lives.

In Book Two of *World Geography and You*, you will study the continents of Africa, Asia, and Australia. You will read about the highest mountains in the world and the longest river in the world. You will read about nations with millions of people and nations where few people live. You will read about places that are very dry and places where it rains often.

As you read, think about how these places are changing. Think about the ways these places will stay the same. Think about how you are different from and how you are like your neighbors on planet Earth.

UNIT
1

The Middle East and North Africa

Dear Aunt Teresa,

Most of this region is hot and dry. Yesterday we saw a big ship carrying oil. The cities are mostly near the ocean and the rivers. They are very crowded.

Love,
Fernando

Teresa Estrada
110 Melrose Avenue
Detroit, Michigan
U.S.A.   48208

جمهورية مصر العربية

Chapter One

The Middle East and North Africa: A Crossroads Region

NEW WORDS

sand dunes
oasis
crossroads
Judaism
Jews
Christianity
Islam
Muslims
nomads

Imagine you are traveling through a huge desert. All you can see is brown land that is covered with dry sand and rocks. The wind is blowing sand into hills called **sand dunes**. The shapes of these dunes change all the time. You also pass brown hills and mountains. There are small plants, but no trees block the sun and wind. You might not see another person for days. After a few days in the desert, you might come to a green grassy field with trees. You see people with herds of goats and sheep. You have come to an **oasis**. An oasis is a place in the middle of the desert where there is water. In this imaginary trip you have just visited the deserts of North Africa and the Middle East.

▶ This oasis is in the middle of the desert.

8

The Middle East and North Africa make up a region that has almost twice as much land as the United States. Find this large region on the map below. Notice the important location of the Middle East. It is part of southwest Asia. To travel by land between Asia and Europe or Africa, people often go through the Middle East. So this area is called a **crossroads**. Some of the roads that go through this region have been used since ancient times.

Notice on the map that this region has several large bodies of water. Many North African nations, and important port cities, are on the Mediterranean Sea. Some Middle Eastern nations also have coasts on this large sea. People in this region use the ocean, the Red and Mediterranean seas, and the Persian Gulf for fishing and trade.

Many landforms can be found in the Middle East and North Africa. There are lowland plains near many coasts. Hills and mountains cover most areas that are

THE MIDDLE EAST AND NORTH AFRICA

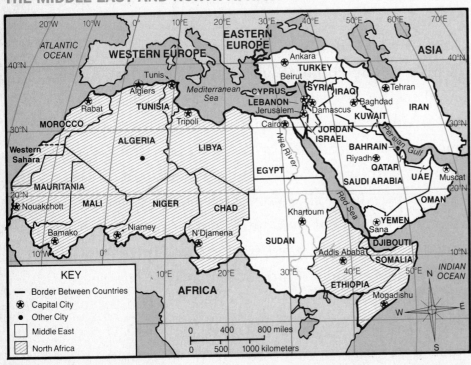

▶ The Atlas Mountains are along the coast of northwest Africa.

away from the coasts. But the Atlas Mountains are along the Mediterranean and Atlantic coasts of northwest Africa. The Atlas Mountains form the longest mountain chain in Africa. Mountains also cover much of Iran and the land near the west coast of Saudi Arabia. A plateau covers the central part of Saudi Arabia. Saudi Arabia is a large peninsula. Mountains, plains, and plateaus also cover the Sahara, the large desert in North Africa.

One of the largest areas of North Africa is the Sahara. The Sahara is the largest desert in the world. Very few people live in this hot, dry land.

Three of the climates you have learned about are found in the Middle East and North Africa. Areas near the Mediterranean Sea have short, rainy winters and long, dry summers. You will remember that this is called a Mediterranean climate. The northern part of the region has a continental climate with very long, cold winters and very short, hot summers. Some areas, such as the Atlas Mountains in northwest Africa, have snowy winters. The Sahara and other parts of the region have a dry desert climate. In some deserts, the temperature at night is 50 degrees lower than it is in the daytime. Most of the Middle East and North Africa gets little rain.

For thousands of years, most people in North Africa and the Middle East have lived near rivers and oases. The region is so dry that many people irrigate their land to be able to grow food. The Nile, Tigris, Euphrates, and Jordan rivers have been important for thousands of years. The soil around these rivers is very fertile. Early settlers in the region built cities along these life-giving rivers.

Oil is the region's most important natural resource. There is more oil in this region than in any other part of the world. Industrial nations all over the world buy millions of barrels of oil from nations in this region each year.

Three of the world's modern religions began in the Middle East. **Judaism**, the religion of the **Jews**, began in what is now Israel. Jews were the first people to believe in one god. Both **Christianity** and **Islam** developed from Judaism. Christians believe that Jesus, who was born about 2000 years ago, was the son of God. Christians follow the teachings of Jesus. About 1400 years ago, Islam began in Saudi Arabia under a leader named Mohammed. People who believe in Islam are called **Muslims**. Today, Muslims are the largest religious group in this region. People from many nations and ethnic groups follow Islam.

◀ This farm is irrigated with water from the Euphrates River.

▶ Most of the Arabs in the Middle East are Muslims.

The region has about 300 million people. They belong to different ethnic groups. About two thirds of the people are Arabs, and most Arabs are Muslims. Other Arabs are Christians. Most of the Jews in the region live in Israel.

People in the Middle East and North Africa have many different ways of living. **Nomads** live in tents and move with their herds from one oasis to another. Most of the region's people live in small, traditional villages. Village farmers work hard to grow food in this dry region. Only a small number of the region's people work in industries. But a few people have become very rich from the oil business. The oil industry is bringing people from all over the world to this crossroads region.

Using What You Learned

Finish each sentence in Group A with an answer from Group B. Write the letter for the correct answer on the line.

Group A

1. A fertile area with water in the desert is an _____.

2. The Middle East and North Africa is called a _____.

3. Many North African nations and important port cities are on the _____.

4. Saudi Arabia is a large _____.

5. The largest desert in the world is the _____.

6. Most of this region gets _____.

7. The region's most important natural resource is _____.

8. In the Middle East and North Africa, Arabs are the largest _____.

9. The largest religious group in the Middle East and North Africa is the _____.

10. People who move from one oasis to another are called _____.

Group B

a. peninsula

b. ethnic group

c. Mediterranean Sea

d. Muslims

e. oasis

f. nomads

g. crossroads

h. Sahara

i. oil

j. very little rain

▼ Think and Apply —— Finding the Main Idea

A **main idea** is an important idea in the chapter. Less important ideas support the main idea. Read each group of sentences below. One of the sentences is a main idea. The other two sentences support the main idea. Write an **M** next to the sentence that is the main idea in each group. The first one is done for you.

1. _____ a. Most people are farmers.

   _____ b. There are not many industries.

   __M__ c. The Middle East and North Africa is a developing region.

2. _____ a. People use the Mediterranean Sea for fishing.

   _____ b. People use the Mediterranean Sea for trade.

   _____ c. The Mediterranean Sea is very important.

3. _____ a. Rivers are important to the Middle East and North Africa.

   _____ b. Long ago, people built cities near rivers.

   _____ c. People use river water to irrigate the land.

4. _____ a. There are lowlands near the coast.

   _____ b. The region has many landforms.

   _____ c. There are mountains, peninsulas, and plateaus.

5. _____ a. Three religions began in the Middle East.

   _____ b. Judaism and Christianity began in what is now Israel.

   _____ c. Islam began in Saudi Arabia.

▼ Skill Builder —— Using Directions on a Political Map

A **compass rose** shows directions on a map. The four main directions are **north**, **south**, **east**, and **west**. The in-between directions are **northeast**, **southeast**, **northwest**, and **southwest**. All directions can be shortened to **N, S, E, W** and **NE, SE, NW,** and **SW**. Write the shortened directions on the compass rose below. Two are done for you.

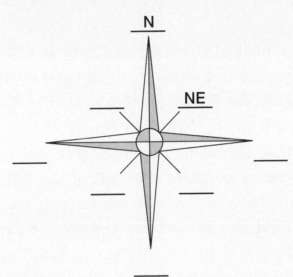

A political map shows the nations of a region. Use the compass rose to finish the sentences about the political map on page 9. Circle the correct word to finish each sentence.

1. _____ is in the northwest of North Africa.

   Egypt   Iran   Morocco

2. Iraq is _____ of Egypt.

   west   southeast   northeast

3. Saudi Arabia is _____ of Iran.

   northwest   northeast   southwest

4. A country in the northeast of the Middle East is _____.

   Jordan   Iran   Turkey

5. Egypt is _____ of the Mediterranean Sea.

   northeast   west   south

Chapter Two

Egypt: The Gift of the Nile

NEW WORDS

mouth
delta
channels
pyramids
silt
dam
hydroelectric power
erosion
disease

Most of the land in Egypt is dry desert where few people live. Nearly all Egyptians live in the north, near the Nile River. So this nation is sometimes called the "gift of the Nile." As you read this chapter, find ways that Egyptians use the river. Try to guess why this nation is called the "gift of the Nile."

The Nile River is the longest river in the world. Find this important waterway on the map on page 17. Notice that the Nile starts 4150 miles away from the Mediterranean Sea in eastern Africa. The river flows from south to north. The Nile empties into the Mediterranean Sea. The place where a river empties into a larger body of water is called its **mouth**.

At its mouth, the Nile forms a **delta**. A delta is a wide area of land in the shape of a triangle. A delta

▶ The Nile River has been important to Egypt for thousands of years.

16

forms where a large river splits into smaller **channels**. Deltas form because rivers carry lots of sand and soil until they come to the mouth. A river flows more slowly when it reaches a larger body of water, such as the Mediterranean Sea. Much of the soil in the river water is left near the mouth of the river where it forms islands. These channels and islands create a delta. Alexandria is an ancient port city built near this Nile Delta.

About 5000 years ago, Egyptians first built cities along the Nile. Many of the buildings from this time still look almost like new. This is because Egypt's dry climate has kept them from being destroyed over time. Some of ancient Egypt's most famous buildings are huge **pyramids**. Workers built these four-sided, triangle-shaped buildings with millions of heavy stone blocks. Today, people from around the world visit the pyramids.

Most Egyptians still live along the Nile today. Almost seven million people live in Cairo, a port city on the Nile. Cairo is also the nation's capital.

EGYPT

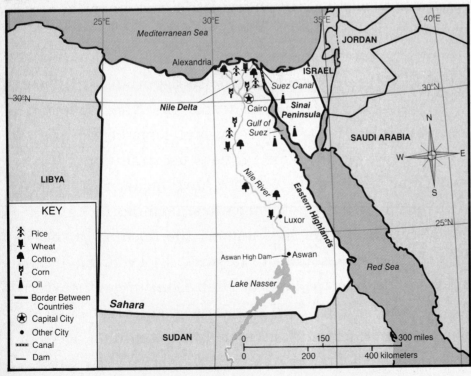

▲ Cairo is the largest city in Egypt.

Egyptians settled on the Nile because they needed its water to grow food. Until 1968, the Nile flooded its valley every summer. Flood waters always left mud and **silt** on the farmland of the Nile Valley. Silt is fertile, wet soil carried by river water. This silt was a natural fertilizer that farmers knew they would get from the Nile every year. Floods made the Nile Valley one of the most fertile areas for farming in the world. Egyptians have also used the Nile to irrigate farms near the rivers for thousands of years.

Some Egyptians work in heavy industries to produce cement, cloth, and steel. But most Egyptians still work as farmers on the fertile land near the Nile. Egyptian farmers grow wheat, rice, corn, and some of the finest cotton in the world. Most farmers use traditional ways of farming because they do not have modern machines.

But even without new machines, farming in Egypt has changed. A **dam** has stopped the flooding of the Nile that was so helpful to farmers. In 1968, Egyptians finished building the Aswan High Dam in southeastern Egypt. South of the dam is a large lake called Lake Nasser. North of the dam, more than 2 million acres of lowlands that were once too dry to farm are irrigated with lake water. Since these fields now have water all through the year, farmers can grow three crops each year. So farmers produce more crops than they could when there was only one flood each year. Egypt earns a lot of money by exporting cotton grown in this area. The Aswan High Dam also makes **hydroelectric power**. Many farming villages now have electricity that is made in power plants near this dam.

But the dam has also caused three problems. First, the Aswan High Dam stops the summer floods that carried silt to fertilize the land. Egyptians must now buy fertilizers to improve the soil. Poor farmers do not have the money to buy these fertilizers. The second problem is **erosion** of the Nile Delta. Erosion means that the land of the Nile Delta is being washed away. The dam stops most of the silt that was once in the flood waters. It keeps the silt in Lake Nasser, so the delta no longer receives new soil from the river. The waves and currents of the Mediterranean Sea are slowly eroding, or washing away, the land at the mouth of the Nile. Third, the dam has caused a sickness to become a problem. Before the dam was built, the Nile

▼ The Aswan High Dam is on the Nile River.

▶ This ship is carrying goods through the Suez Canal.

floods killed tiny snails that carried a stomach **disease**. Flood waters no longer kill the snails, and now many Egyptians get this stomach disease because they use the Nile's water for drinking and washing.

Not all Egyptians live along the Nile. Some Egyptians live on the Sinai Peninsula. The Sinai Peninsula is east of the Suez Canal. This region has helped Egypt in two important ways. First, Egypt earns money from shipping on the Suez Canal. Egypt controls this canal. The Suez Canal makes trade easier among Europe, Africa, and Asia. The canal connects the Mediterranean Sea and the Red Sea. So the canal is a shortcut between these two big bodies of water. Every ship must pay money to Egypt to use this shortcut. Each year, Egypt earns large amounts of money from shipping on the canal. Second, the nation has oil fields in the Sinai Peninsula. The nation earns money by exporting its oil.

Egypt is a developing nation with a population that is growing very fast. Today, Egypt has about 55 million people. Most of these people are Muslim Arabs.

Today, Egyptians are building modern factories and schools instead of pyramids. But Egyptians still depend on the Nile River in many ways.

Using What You Learned

▼ Read and Remember —— Finish the Story

Use the words in dark print to finish the story. Write the words you choose on the correct blanks.

Mediterranean Sea	**desert**	**Cairo**
Egypt	**Africa**	**delta**

The Nile River begins in eastern _____. It flows north through

_____. The Nile flows into the _____. At the sea, the

Nile forms a _____ in the shape of a triangle. Most Egyptians live

on the land around the Nile. The rest of Egypt is a huge _____.

Egypt's capital city, _____, is a port on the Nile River.

▼ Skill Builder —— Reading a Resource Map

Resource maps show where resources can be found in an area. Some resource maps can show where minerals are found or which crops are grown. Look at the resource map on page 17. Use the map key to find out which resources are shown. Then circle the word to finish each sentence.

1. A resource in the Sinai Peninsula is _____.

   wheat   oil   corn

2. A product from the Nile Valley is _____.

   cotton   wool   oil

3. A food crop from the southern part of the Nile Valley is _____.

   oil   rice   wheat

4. A resource that might be shipped through the Suez Canal to the Mediterranean is _____.

   oil   cotton   rice

Read the first two sentences below. Then read the third sentence. Notice how it follows from the first two sentences. The third sentence is called a **conclusion**.

> The Sinai Peninsula has oil.
> The Sinai Peninsula has the Suez Canal.

Conclusion: The Sinai Peninsula is important to Egypt.

Read each pair of sentences. Then look in the box for the conclusion you can make. Write the letter of the conclusion on the blank. The first one is done for you.

1. Thousands of years ago, Egyptians used the Nile River to irrigate their land.
   Long ago, Egyptians built cities near the Nile.

   Conclusion __c__

2. The Aswan High Dam saves water in Lake Nasser.
   The Aswan High Dam uses water power to make electricity.

   Conclusion _____

3. Egypt has almost no rain.
   Most of Egypt is covered with desert.

   Conclusion _____

4. The Aswan High Dam stops silt from fertilizing the soil.
   The Aswan High Dam has caused a disease to be a problem.

   Conclusion _____

   a. The Aswan High Dam helps Egyptians make better use of the Nile River.
   b. The Aswan High Dam has caused problems in Egypt.
   c. The Nile was important to Egyptians long ago.
   d. Egyptians need the Nile to grow food in their desert climate.

Chapter Three

Israel: A Nation of Jews and Arabs

NEW WORDS

holy
sea level
kibbutz
percent
homeland
international
United Nations
defeat

Israel is a desert nation that is home to both Arabs and Jews. In this chapter, you will learn how Israelis have fought to control their small nation. You will also learn how Israelis have worked to develop a nation in a land with few resources.

Find Israel on the map below. Notice that Israel touches both the Mediterranean Sea and the Red Sea. Israel also has borders with four Arab nations. Find each of these nations.

Most of Israel has a warm, Mediterranean climate. This climate is good for industries and farms on the coastal plains near the Mediterranean Sea. Tel Aviv, the nation's largest city and a big industrial center, is on this coastal plain.

ISRAEL

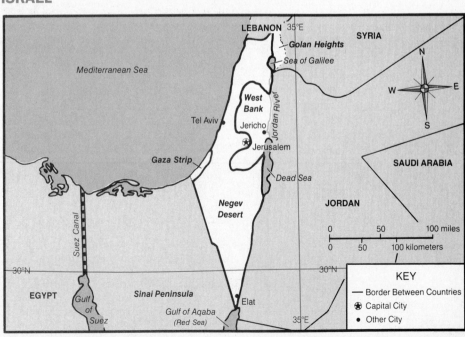

23

Highlands cover most of the land that is east of the coastal plain. This highland area has hills and mountains. The Sea of Galilee is in this northern part of Israel. Pipelines carry water from the Sea of Galilee to drier parts of Israel. Jerusalem, the capital of Israel, is also in these highlands. People of three religions have special places to pray in Jerusalem. So Jerusalem is a **holy** city for Christians, Jews, and Muslims.

The southern part of Israel has a dry desert climate. The driest part of Israel is the Negev Desert. Animals graze on the plains and hills of this desert. And some desert farmers irrigate with water from the Sea of Galilee. The Rift Valley is east of the Negev Desert. This valley is a giant crack in Earth's crust. A saltwater lake called the Dead Sea is in this area. The Dead Sea is the lowest place on Earth. The surface of this sea is 1310 feet lower than the surface of the ocean. So the Dead Sea is 1310 feet below **sea level**.

Israel has few resources. Israel has little water and few minerals. The nation gets salt and minerals from the Dead Sea. These resources are used to make fertilizers and chemicals. Israel has to import all the

▶ Jerusalem is the capital of Israel.

24

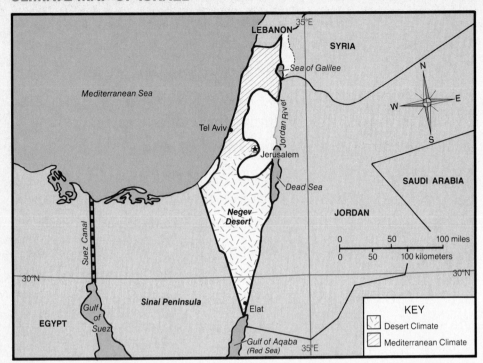

other raw materials it needs for industry. The nation also has borrowed money from developed nations. With this help, Israelis have developed farms and industries.

Food products, cloth, and clothes are important factory goods. Diamonds are imported, cut and polished, and then exported. Industries also make building materials, military equipment, computers, and machines. About half the factories are privately owned. The rest are owned by labor unions and the government.

Even with the desert climate, Israeli farmers grow about three fourths of the food that the nation needs. Oranges, eggs, milk, and chickens are Israel's most important farm products. To have good farms, Israelis have drained water out of swamps. And they have irrigated dry areas. Israelis are teaching farmers in developing nations how to make their farms better.

Much of Israel's food is grown on **kibbutz** farms. A kibbutz is an Israeli community with farms and businesses owned by all of the members. Members share the work, machines, and money earned by the kibbutz. Members eat together, like a large family.

About four and a half million people live in Israel. About 83 **percent**, or 83 out of 100, Israelis are Jews. Since the nation was created in 1948, almost 2 million Jews have moved there from Europe, Africa, and Asia. About 16 percent of the population is Arab. Most Arabs live in farming villages or in Arab neighborhoods in cities. In many places, Israeli Arabs and Jews live and work together with no problems.

Jews lived in the land that is now Israel for thousands of years. They saw it as the **homeland** promised to their people by God. But about 2000 years ago their land was taken by the Romans, and after that by the Arabs. The land became known as Palestine. Most of the Jews who lived there moved to other places.

Jews around the world dreamed of returning to Palestine and having an independent country there again. About a hundred years ago, they began to make this dream come true. Many Jews from Europe moved to Palestine. They built new cities and farmed the land. During World War II, the German Nazis killed about 6 million Jews. So many more Jews left Europe and moved to Palestine.

But the Arabs who lived in Palestine did not want the

▶ This boy lives and works on a kibbutz in Israel.

◀ Many Jews moved to Palestine after World War II.

Jews to control the land. The Palestinian Arabs said that the country was theirs. But the Jews said that they had a right to the land. The Jews and Arabs in Palestine could not agree on who would rule the country. In 1947, an **international** government called the **United Nations**, or UN, voted that Palestine be divided into two separate states, one Jewish and the other Arab. The Jews accepted the idea, but the Arabs did not. In 1948, the Jews set up their own state called Israel. The neighboring Arab countries attacked it but could not **defeat** it.

Israel and the Arab countries have fought four wars since 1948. In the 1967 war, Israel took control of the West Bank of the Jordan River and the Gaza Strip. These are parts of old Palestine. The people who live in them are Palestinian Arabs who do not want to be part of Israel. They want to have their own state. There are talks between the Israelis and Arabs to decide what should be done with the West Bank and Gaza Strip.

Because of the fighting with the Arabs, Israel has to spend a lot of money on its army. Still, it has been able to build a strong and modern country.

Using What You Learned

▼ **Read and Remember —— Finish Up**

Choose a word in dark print to finish each sentence. Write the words you choose on the correct blank.

| **Jerusalem** | **raw materials** | **sea level** | **kibbutz** |
| **Mediterranean** | **farm products** | **minerals** | **Sea of Galilee** |

1. Israel touches the _____ sea and the Red Sea.

2. The city of _____ is holy to Christians, Muslims, and Jews.

3. Pipelines carry water from the _____ to drier parts of Israel.

4. The Dead Sea is 1310 feet below _____.

5. Israelis use salt and _____ from the Dead Sea to make fertilizer.

6. Israel spends a lot of money importing _____.

7. Oranges, eggs, milk, and chickens are important _____.

8. The people of a _____ farm share their work, tools, and profits.

▼ **Skill Builder —— Using a Climate Map**

   Climate maps help you learn about the weather in an area. They show which areas are rainy and which areas are dry. Climate maps help you learn which places are hot and which are cold.

   The map key on the climate map on page 25 shows two different climates. Israel's desert climate has hot summers, mild winters, and almost no rain. A Mediterranean climate has hot, dry summers and cool, rainy winters.

Look at the climate map. Then write **T** next to each sentence that is true. Write **F** next to each sentence that is false.

_____ 1. The land in northern Israel has a Mediterranean climate.

_____ 2. The city of Tel Aviv has a desert climate.

_____ 3. The city of Elat has rainy winters.

_____ 4. The city of Jerusalem has a desert climate.

_____ 5. The land near the Sea of Galilee has hot, dry summers and cool, rainy winters.

▼ Think and Apply —— Cause and Effect

A **cause** is something that makes something else happen. What happens is called an **effect**.

Cause	Effect
Many tourists visit Israel, so	many Israelis work in tourist businesses.

Match each **cause** on the left with an **effect** on the right. Write the letter of the effect on the correct blank. The first one is done for you.

Cause

1. Israel has few natural resources, so __d__.

2. Israel has little water, so _____.

3. The southern part of Israel is very dry, so _____.

4. Arabs do not want Jews to control the West Bank, so _____.

5. Millions of Jews were killed in World War II, so _____.

6. Israel does not have peace with most Arab nations, so _____.

Effect

a. pipelines carry water there from the Sea of Galilee.

b. there are talks about who should control the West Bank.

c. Israel needs a large army.

d. the nation imports many resources.

e. farmers use water carefully.

f. many Jews moved to their homeland.

Chapter Four

The Persian Gulf Nations: Land of Oil

NEW WORDS

strait
oil tankers
Fertile Crescent
crude oil
oil refineries
petrochemicals

More than half of the world's known supply of oil is in the eight nations that surround the Persian Gulf. This important resource has made the region rich and powerful. In this chapter, you will learn about the land, climate, and religion of these oil-rich nations.

Find the Persian Gulf on the map on page 31. Notice that this body of water is connected to the Indian Ocean. Find the narrow part of the Persian Gulf near the Indian Ocean. This narrow waterway is called a **strait**. Its name is the Strait of Hormuz. The strait is important to the region because large ships called **oil tankers** pass through it. So all eight nations want the strait to be open. If a nation blocks the strait, it is hard for oil to get to other nations that depend on it.

▶ This ship from Iran is carrying oil.

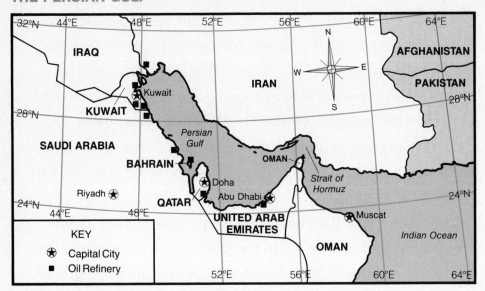

Now find the eight nations that have a coast on the Persian Gulf. Iran and Iraq are on the north side of the gulf. The other six nations share the dry Arabian Peninsula that is south and west of the gulf. The largest nation in the region, Saudi Arabia, has a western border on the Red Sea.

As you travel across the region, you notice that most nations have a desert climate. Sometimes no rain falls for several months or even years. No rivers or lakes hold water above ground during the year. So many people depend on the few oases with their water. Saudi Arabia's capital, Riyadh, was built around an oasis in the desert. Some parts of Iran have a continental climate and receive some rain. The part of Iran near the Caspian Sea has a Mediterranean climate with rainy winters.

Many kinds of landforms are found in this region. On the Arabian Peninsula, there are windy deserts and dry mountains. There are lowlands near the Persian Gulf. In Iran, there is a plateau in the middle of the nation. Iran also has high mountains with a desert climate. A few streams in the mountains have enough water to irrigate crops. But most people who live in the mountains herd goats and sheep.

Iraq, to the west, also has high mountains and deserts. But a few parts of this nation have water and fertile soil. Two important rivers, the Tigris and the Euphrates, flow through Iraq. Farmers have used the rivers for irrigation for over 5000 years. Fertile plains in the river valleys produce much more food than the deserts can. So this area is called the **Fertile Crescent**. The Fertile Crescent goes from the Mediterranean Sea to the Persian Gulf. But only a small part of the land in the whole Persian Gulf region is fertile.

Over the past 35 years, many people moved from the farms and villages to the growing towns and cities. Fewer than one out of three people are now farmers. Some farmers use modern farm machines, fertilizers, and irrigation. But many still do not have modern tools. Farmers grow grains, beans, vegetables, fruit, and cotton. Dates, olives, and grapes are grown here, too.

About two thirds of the people live and work in the growing towns and cities. Most of the region's money comes from oil. Oil is the most important resource in the Persian Gulf region. Modern machines drill into the ground for **crude oil**. It is sent to **oil refineries,** where

▶ Some people in the Persian Gulf region are still traditional farmers.

chemicals are removed. The chemicals are called **petrochemicals**. These petrochemicals are used to make products such as plastic. Pipelines carry oil to ports on the Persian Gulf, the Mediterranean Sea, and the Red Sea. At these ports, oil tankers are filled with oil. Then the tankers carry the oil to nations around the world.

Six nations of the Persian Gulf formed a group with seven other oil-rich nations from other parts of the world. These 13 nations are a group called OPEC. These nations have almost three fourths of the world's oil supply. All the nations of OPEC sell their oil for the same price. OPEC has been a very powerful group.

Most of the people of the Persian Gulf nations are Arabs who speak Arabic. But the people of Iran are Persians. Most of the people in this region are Muslims who follow Islam. Muslims believe in one god called Allah. Muslims believe that Allah spoke to people through a man named Mohammed. Islam began with Mohammed's teaching in the Saudi Arabian city of Mecca. So all Muslims try to visit the holy city of Mecca

▲ Petrochemicals are removed from crude oil at this refinery.

33

at least once in their life. Muslims pray at least five times each day. Muslims believe that all people should help care for poor people.

Islam has rules for people's daily lives. Muslims may not eat pork or drink alcohol. Islam treats men and women differently. In some of these nations, Muslim women must cover their faces and hair when they leave their homes. The governments of Iran and Saudi Arabia follow the laws of Islam closely.

Persian Gulf nations share the religion, landforms, climates, and resources of the region. But all the people in the region do not share in the riches that come from oil. Nations have used their oil money to build schools, roads, factories, and hospitals. And some people have a high standard of living. But oil money has not helped all people who live around the Persian Gulf.

▶ Some Muslim women must cover their faces and hair when they leave their homes.

Using What You Learned

▼ **Read and Remember —— True or False**

Write **T** next to each sentence that is true. Write **F** next to each sentence that is false. There are three false sentences. On the lines below, rewrite the false sentences to make them true.

_____ 1. Eight nations on the Persian Gulf are rich in oil.

_____ 2. The people of Iraq use the Tigris and Euphrates rivers to irrigate their farmland.

_____ 3. There are many lakes and rivers in Saudi Arabia.

_____ 4. All nations of the Persian Gulf have a Mediterranean climate.

_____ 5. Less than half of the world's oil supply is in the Persian Gulf region.

_____ 6. The Strait of Hormuz connects the Persian Gulf with the Indian Ocean.

_____ 7. Oil leaves the Persian Gulf in huge tankers.

_____

_____

_____

▼ **Skill Builder —— Reading a Political Map**

Look at the political map of the Persian Gulf on page 31. Notice that the map also shows oil refineries. Use the map to answer these questions.

1. Name the eight countries that have borders on the Persian Gulf.

_____

_____

2. Which nation has the most oil refineries? _____

3. What two countries border the Strait of Hormuz? _____

_____

4. Which nation is an island? _____

_____

5. Name two capital cities on the Persian Gulf. _____

_____

▼ **Think and Apply —— Categories**

Read the words about the Persian Gulf in each group. Decide how they are alike. Find the best title for each group in the box. Write the title on the line above each group. The first one is done for you.

Three Nations Using Oil Money	**Bodies of Water Three Climates**	**Islam Needed in Oil Business**

1. **Three Nations**
   Kuwait
   Oman
   Iraq

2. _____
   drilling machines
   oil refineries
   oil tankers

3. _____
   Persian Gulf
   Strait of Hormuz
   Tigris River

4. _____
   new schools
   new factories
   new hospitals

5. _____
   pray five times each day
   care for poor people
   visit Mecca

6. _____
   desert
   Mediterranean
   continental

Chapter Five

Problems in the Middle East and North Africa

NEW WORDS

poverty

average income

distilling

peace treaty

refugees

citizens

civil war

▼ Poverty is a big problem in the Middle East and North Africa.

The Middle East and North Africa have the largest oil fields in the world. This region earns billions of dollars every year by selling oil to developed nations. But this region still has problems. In this chapter you will learn about five of these problems.

Most nations in the Persian Gulf region and along the Mediterranean coast have raised their standard of living with their oil money or modern industries. But many people in the Middle East and North Africa live in **poverty**. In parts of North Africa, most people are still poor farmers and herders.

You can tell how high a nation's standard of living is if you know the **average income**. To find the average income, you add up all the money earned in that nation

in a year. Then you divide that number by the nation's population. In Kuwait, the average person earns more than $16,000 a year. But in Egypt, the average income is only $640. So oil money has not helped everyone.

The problem of poverty is hard to solve. Poor people must often rent land at high prices because they do not have enough money to buy a farm. The poor often spend very few years in school. They spend most of their time doing farm work. Many nations do not have enough schools. So many people do not have enough skills to get better jobs. They remain poor farmers. Some oil companies and nations are building new schools. Some nations in the Middle East and North Africa send students to other nations to learn needed skills. But poverty is still a serious problem in much of the region.

The second problem is that these desert nations do not have much water and fertile land. Most nations cannot grow enough food to feed all their people. Every year, these nations spend millions of dollars to import food.

Nations are trying to solve this problem in different ways. Egypt uses water from Lake Nasser to irrigate millions of acres of dry land. Israelis have also turned deserts into farms that grow about three fourths of the

▼ These children go to school in Turkey.

◀ Many farmers in the Middle East are learning to irrigate land in the desert.

food its people need. In Saudi Arabia, farmers are using irrigation at oases. Modern machines help them to grow more food than ever before. In Morocco, farmers plant crops in fertile land in the bottoms of lakes that are dry for part of the year.

Some nations, such as Kuwait, cannot irrigate because they do not have any rivers and lakes. And the water from underground wells is too salty to drink. Before 1950, Kuwait imported its drinking water from Iraq. But in 1950, Kuwaitis began **distilling** sea water to take out the salt. Today, Kuwait's distilling factories produce millions of gallons of drinking water every day. Kuwait has also found some fresh water underground. But most of the water Kuwait needs comes from distilleries.

Fighting between Israelis and Arabs is a third problem in the Middle East. Israel now controls land that was once Palestine, including land that belongs to Arab nations. But Arabs want their land back. Some also want all the land that the UN voted to be the state of Israel. To make things worse, Muslim Arabs and Jewish Israelis do not have the same religion. Many on each side think their own religion is better. Since 1948, Arab nations and Israel have fought four more wars. In these wars, Israel took land from Syria, Jordan, Egypt, and Lebanon.

Part of this land is called the Occupied Territories because Israel controls the land with soldiers. In 1979, Egypt and Israel signed a **peace treaty**. Egypt and Israel promised not to attack each other. Israel returned land that belonged to Egypt.

But there is still fighting between some Palestinians and Israelis. The Palestinians are Arabs who lived in Palestine before 1948. Palestinians want their own nation in the Middle East. They formed a group to speak and act for them. It is called the Palestine Liberation Organization (PLO).

Palestinian **refugees** are the fourth problem in this region. Palestinian refugees left their homes and went to other Arab nations during the Arab-Israeli wars. Refugees now live in the Occupied Territories and Arab nations. Many Palestinians are not allowed to become

▶ The leaders of Egypt and Israel signed a peace treaty in 1979.

citizens of the Arab nations in which they now live. To solve this problem, leaders from both sides must talk about fair ways to treat these people who want a safe home.

▲ Many people lost their homes during the war in Kuwait.

Wars in other parts of the Middle East are the fifth problem. Other nations in the Middle East do not get along. War broke out between Iran and Iraq in 1980. This war lasted about eight years. And there has been **civil war** inside Lebanon since 1975. Five different religious and ethnic groups are fighting to win control of that small nation's government.

In 1990, Iraq and Kuwait got into an argument about oil prices and oil wells. Troops from Iraq attacked Kuwait. They took over Kuwait and its valuable oil wells. In 1991, American and Western European troops joined forces with many Arab nations. Together they attacked and defeated Iraq. Kuwait was freed from Iraq.

The Middle East and North Africa have problems of poverty, a small water supply, and disagreements among people and nations. If the nations of the region can come to peace, they may be able to solve the other problems of this region together.

Using What You Learned

▼ **Think and Apply —— Analogies**

An **analogy** compares two pairs of words. The words in the first pair are alike in the same way as the words in the second pair. For example, the **Israelis** are to **Israel** as the **Egyptians** are to **Egypt**. Use a word in dark print to finish each sentence. The first one is done for you.

Jerusalem	**Lebanon**	**Morocco**	**Egypt**
developing nations	**irrigation**	**Nile River**	

1. Developed nations are to Western Europe as **developing nations** are to the Middle East and North Africa.

2. Iran is to the Middle East as _____ is to North Africa.

3. The Tigris River is to Iraq as the _____ is to Egypt.

4. Arab-Israeli wars are to the Middle East as civil war is to _____.

5. Mecca is to Saudi Arabia as _____ is to Israel.

6. Kuwait is to distilling as Saudi Arabia is to _____.

7. The Atlas Mountains are to North Africa as the Sinai Peninsula is to _____.

▼ **Read and Remember —— Find the Answer**

Put a check (✔) next to the sentences below that tell about problems in the Middle East and North Africa today. You should check five sentences.

_____ 1. The region does not have enough oil.

_____ 2. There is not enough water and fertile land.

_____ 3. There have been wars between the Israelis and the Arabs.

_____ 4. The Aswan High Dam is too large.

_____ 5. There are problems with Palestinian refugees.

_____ 6. There are too many nations in the region.

_____ 7. There was a long war between Iran and Iraq.

_____ 8. Many people have a low standard of living.

▼ Skill Builder —— Comparing Landform Maps

Look at the **landform maps** of Saudi Arabia and Turkey below. A landform map shows the landforms of a nation. Use the map key to find the kinds of landforms in the nations of Turkey and Saudi Arabia.

TURKEY

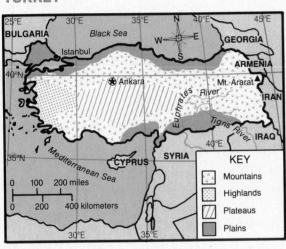

SAUDI ARABIA

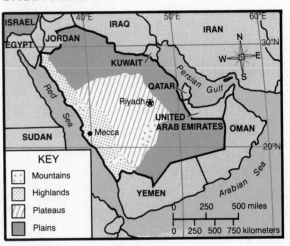

Finish each sentence with the word **Turkey** or **Saudi Arabia**.

1. Eastern _____ has lots of mountains.

2. Eastern _____ has large areas of plains.

3. The western part of _____ is highlands and mountains.

4. Of the two countries, _____ has more mountains.

5. There are many mountains along the southern coast of _____.

6. There are highlands along the western coast of _____.

43

Bedouin and Oases

The traveler sees a tent in the distance. Around it stand camels and goats. As he comes closer, he sees that a motorcycle is parked near the tent. From inside the tent comes the sound of music over a radio.

People come out of the tent when the traveler arrives. A bearded man dressed in long robes invites the traveler inside. There women with covered faces serve tea.

The traveler has entered the world of the Bedouin. It is a world caught between the old and the new.

▲ These Bedouin live in Israel.

Location/Place

The Bedouin live in the deserts of Saudi Arabia and other nations. For hundreds of years, the Bedouin people have lived in the desert. The word Bedouin means "camel herder." The Bedouin call themselves the true Arabs.

The land of the Bedouin is hot and dry. Much of it is covered with sand. Little rain falls, and few plants grow. The only water is found in wells. Date palm trees often grow near these wells. The Bedouin visit the oases to water their animals.

Human/Environment Interaction

The Bedouin make the most of the few resources of their land. Camels can go for several days without water. They are used to carry goods across the desert. Today, though, more and more Bedouin use pickup trucks.

The Bedouin know how to survive in the desert. They get milk and meat from camels. Camel hair is made into cloth for tents. Dates found at oases are also eaten.

Family and honor are very important to the Bedouin. Family and honor help them survive in the hot, dry desert.

Movement

Travel was once a way of life for the Bedouin. They moved their animals from one oasis to another to get food and water. They couldn't survive in the desert without the oases.

Long ago, the Bedouin were important in trade between different parts of the world. Large groups of their camels carried silks, spices, ivory, gold, and other goods across the desert.

Today, few goods are carried across the desert. The Bedouin way of life is changing. Many now live in villages or towns. The Bedouin way of life is quickly disappearing.

▲ Many Bedouin depend on oases for food and water.

Write About It

You are the leader of a band of Bedouin. Part of your tribe wants to move near a city and settle down. Children can go to school. People can find jobs in the city. Other people in your tribe want to keep on living the way the Bedouin have always lived. What would you decide? Write a paragraph telling what you would decide, and why.

_____

_____

_____

_____

_____

Africa South of the Sahara

Dear Mom and Dad,
The cities in Africa are
modern and very crowded.
But most of the people
live in small villages. The
weather has been hot and
dry. Yesterday we saw
giraffes, elephants, and
zebras up close!
        Love, Chan

Lok and Chiang Lee
212 Harker Street
New York City, N.Y.
    U.S.A. 10021

RSA 30c

Chapter Six

Africa South of the Sahara

NEW WORDS

wildlife
basins
savanna
droughts
foreign
plantations
cash crops
subsistence
farmers

What kinds of **wildlife**, or plants and animals, would you find if you visited Africa south of the Sahara? You would see lions, monkeys, giraffes, and crocodiles. You would find birds of many sizes and colors. And you would see many kinds of trees. Parts of this region have short grasses. Other parts have tall, tropical trees with large green leaves. All of this wildlife makes Africa a beautiful place to visit.

Africa is also rich in resources. But it is hard to have a high standard of living on this large continent. All African nations, except one, are developing nations. In this chapter, you will learn how land, climate, and history have made it hard for Africa to develop.

Find Africa on the map on page 49. Notice that Africa is between two oceans. Africa has a long, smooth coast. So it has few harbors. Now find the Sahara on the map. In this chapter, you will study Africa south of this desert. This region is called sub-Saharan Africa.

▼ Tourists visit Africa to see the wildlife.

Most of sub-Saharan Africa is a giant plateau. The plateau is surrounded by narrow coastal plains. A few mountains rise above the plateau. Kilimanjaro, in eastern Africa, is the highest mountain in Africa. Kilimanjaro is so tall that it always has snow at the top.

Five large **basins** are in the plateau. These basins are low areas of land. All the basins are at least 600 miles across and are almost a mile deep.

The Great Rift Valley is a landform in east Africa that is more than 4000 miles long. It goes through most of eastern Africa and into the Middle East. This valley is made of wide, deep cracks in Earth's surface. Many lakes are in the Great Rift Valley in Africa.

Another important area is the Sahel. The Sahel is a dry plain on the south side of the Sahara. Most of the plain is covered with a grassland called a **savanna**. Nomads use the savanna to feed their goats, sheep, and cattle. The Sahel usually gets more rain than the Sahara. But sometimes parts of the Sahel do not receive

AFRICA SOUTH OF THE SAHARA

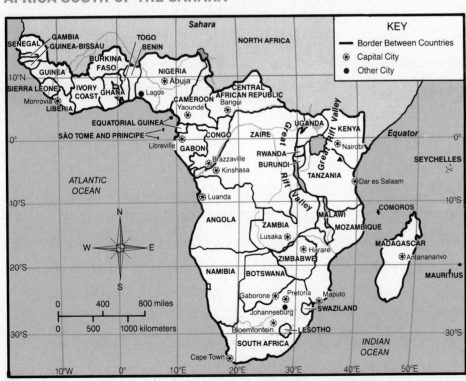

▲ This woman lives in a dry region in Africa.

rain for several years. The times with little or no rain are called **droughts**. You will learn about the problems caused by these droughts in Chapter 10.

There are many kinds of climate in sub-Saharan Africa. The Equator passes through Africa. So that area receives a lot of sunlight and heat. Most of the land near the Equator is hot and rainy and has tropical rain forests. The climate gets drier as you go away from the Equator. Many parts of Africa, such as the savannas in the Sahel, do not get much rain. There are also large deserts in some parts of Africa.

South of the Sahara most people travel in traditional ways. Africa's many rivers are too shallow and rocky for boats. It is difficult to build roads in rain forests and deserts. So most village people travel on foot. In the desert, people travel on camels. Poor transportation makes it hard for African nations to have much trade with one another. People use the food and resources that they can grow or find near their homes.

By the 1900s, Africa's transportation started to become more modern. This happened because people from **foreign** nations wanted Africa's resources. The continent has oil, gold, diamonds, lumber, and many kinds of metals. Africa has land that can be used for **plantations**. Plantations are very large farms. Foreigners wanted to use the land to grow **cash crops**. Cash crops are sold to earn money. Plantations usually grow only one cash crop. Coffee, sugar cane, and cotton are cash crops in Africa.

At first, Europeans traded with Africans. Later, European nations took over parts of Africa. These foreign nations made most of the continent into colonies. People from the ruling nations moved to Africa. These foreigners set up schools, churches, and hospitals in Africa. The Africans mined and produced resources for their ruling nations. African colonies had to export their resources to the ruling nations. African colonies could not export these resources without modern transportation. So foreign nations helped Africans build railroads to carry these resources. Foreign nations also built modern ports on the oceans.

Today, African nations are free to rule themselves. But Africans still depend on the money they earn by exporting resources. Africans are also starting to build factories in their own nations.

◄ Most people who live south of the Sahara use traditional ways of travel.

51

Most Africans are subsistence farmers who live in small villages.

Most Africans today are farmers who grow food crops in gardens. Farmers who grow only enough food for their families are called **subsistence farmers**. Some subsistence farmers would like to grow more food. It is hard for them because they do not have good tools and the soil is not fertile. Modern fertilizers cost too much for most subsistence farmers. Many farmers cannot grow all the kinds of food they need to stay healthy.

Most Africans live in villages. Most villages have small houses made of materials from nature, such as mud, sticks, clay, and grass. Today one African out of four lives in a city. Cities are crowded with people who are looking for work in the government and in factories.

There are over 800 ethnic groups in sub-Saharan Africa. Most Africans are blacks who belong to different ethnic groups. Blacks have lived in Africa for thousands of years. Today there are still white Africans from Europe. There are also Africans from Asia and India.

In the next chapters you will learn about three different African nations. As you read, try to find the ways that these nations are different from one another.

▼ **Read and Remember —— Write the Answer**

Write an answer for each question.

1. Africa is between what two oceans?

_____

_____

2. Where is the Great Rift Valley?

_____

_____

3. What is the Sahel?

_____

_____

4. What is a drought?

_____

_____

5. What are some of Africa's resources?

_____

_____

6. What is subsistence farming?

_____

_____

7. Why did foreign nations want to rule Africa?

_____

_____

▼ Think and Apply —— Exclusions

One word in each group does not belong. Find that word, and cross it out. Then write a sentence that tells how the other words are alike. The first one is done for you.

1. coffee

   cotton

   sugar cane

   ~~wheat~~

   Coffee, cotton, and sugar cane

   are grown as cash crops on plantations.

2. peninsulas

   plateaus

   coastal plains

   basins

3. savannas

   ice and snow

   droughts

   south of the Sahara

4. desert climate

   tropical climate

   Mediterranean climate

   hot and dry climate

5. diamonds

   gold

   oil

   hydroelectric power

A **table** lists groups of facts. Tables are used to learn facts quickly. It is easy to compare facts in a table. Read the table below. Then write the answer to each question.

Facts About Nigeria, Kenya, and South Africa					
Nation	**Location in Africa**	**Which nation ruled it?**	**When did it become free?**	**Largest city**	**Population of largest city**
Nigeria	West Africa	Great Britain	1960	Lagos	1,100,000
Kenya	East Africa	Great Britain	1963	Nairobi	1,000,000
South Africa	Southern Africa	Great Britain	1910	Johannesburg	1,700,000

1. Which European nation ruled all three African nations?

   _____

2. Which city has the largest population?

   _____

3. Where is Kenya?

   _____

4. Which city has the smallest population?

   _____

5. Which nation was first to become a free nation?

   _____

6. Which nation was last to become a free nation?

   _____

Chapter Seven

Nigeria: An Oil-Rich Nation in West Africa

NEW WORDS

swamp
trade partners
consumer goods

▼ Oil is an important export for Nigeria.

The 1960s were a time of great change for Nigeria. Nigeria had been a British colony since 1861. In 1960, Nigeria became a nation that ruled itself. During the 1960s, Nigerians from different ethnic groups fought to control their new nation. There were also changes in the way Nigeria earned most of its money. For many years, the nation earned little money from mining. During the 1960s, oil was discovered near the Gulf of Guinea. Since then, Nigeria has earned most of its money by exporting oil. In this chapter, you will learn about the land and people of this changing, oil-rich nation.

Nigeria is a hot, tropical nation in west Africa. Find this nation on the map below. Notice that the southern border of Nigeria is on the Gulf of Guinea. Some of this coastal land is soft, wet, **swamp** land. Southern Nigeria gets lots of rain and has tropical rain forests. Northern Nigeria is hotter and drier than the south. Dry savannas of the Sahel cover much of the north.

Nigeria gets its name from the Niger River. The Niger flows through a valley that has grasslands, swamps, and forests of palm trees. Find the Niger on the map below. The Niger forms a mud and sand delta at its mouth on the Gulf of Guinea. The Niger and other rivers help Nigeria. Nigerians make hydroelectric power from their rivers. The rivers are used for fishing and transportation.

NIGERIA

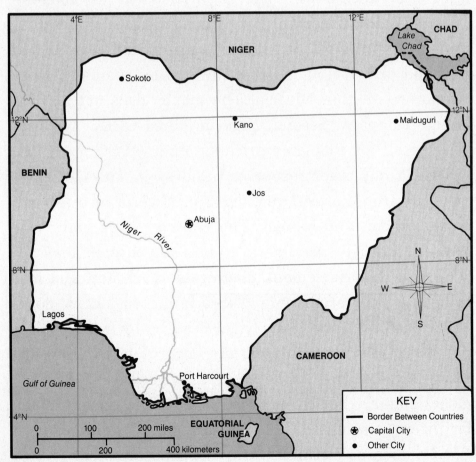

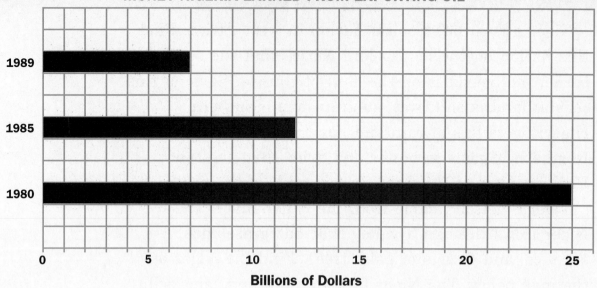

Nigeria earns most of its money by exporting oil. This is both good and bad for Nigeria. It is good because oil has brought much wealth to Nigeria. But it is bad for a nation to depend on just one main resource to earn most of its money. If Nigeria sells less oil, or if the price of oil goes down, Nigeria earns much less money.

In 1971, the Nigerian government did two things to protect its oil. First, it set up a national oil company to find and drill for oil. With a national oil company, more oil money stays in Nigeria. The money does not go to a foreign company. Second, Nigeria joined OPEC. Nigeria sells its oil for the same price as other OPEC members.

Nigeria has other resources besides oil. The nation has coal, iron, natural gas, and tin. Nigeria also exports cocoa, rubber, and lumber. The United States and Western Europe are Nigeria's main **trade partners**.

Nigeria imports cement, chemicals, machines, and food from these trade partners. These imported factory goods and foods cost more than Nigeria earns by selling oil and other raw materials. So the government wants to start new factories inside Nigeria. Nigeria is using oil money to start heavy industries that make cement, steel, fertilizers, and metals. Factories also make **consumer goods**, such as clothing, cars, and food products.

Most Nigerian factories are in urban areas. Only one fourth of the people live in cities, but the cities are growing fast. Lagos was the capital of Nigeria. It is a port on the Gulf of Guinea and the largest industrial city. It now has over one million people. Lagos has many modern factories and tall buildings. But the city also has crowded slums. To help the crowding in Lagos, the government is building a new capital, Abuja, in central Nigeria. Find Abuja on the map on page 57. There are mines for many metals and minerals near Abuja. The government hopes that many people will want to move to the new city.

Nigeria has used its oil money to become a more developed nation. To be able to develop, Nigeria needs many people who have studied in school for many years. When Nigeria was a colony, only one black ethnic group called the Ibo had good schools. So the Ibo had many good jobs in government and business. Other groups of blacks did not think it was fair for the Ibo to have the best schools and jobs. Since 1975, the nation has built many new schools and universities for the many ethnic groups in Nigeria.

▼ Lagos is a crowded, busy city in Nigeria.

▶ Nigeria has the largest population of any country in Africa.

Nigeria has the largest population in Africa. About 120 million people live there. Most Nigerians are farmers who use traditional ways of farming in small gardens. The government has started programs to help these farmers grow more food. But today, Nigeria must still import food to feed its growing population.

Who are the people of Nigeria? Almost all Nigerians are blacks. They belong to more than 250 ethnic groups. About half of the people are Muslims. Most Muslims live in the north. They live a lot like people in the Middle East. Most other people are Christians. Other people follow traditional African religions.

Nigerians have made many changes since 1960. They are free from the control of foreign nations. Oil has become an important business. Nigerians today are using their oil money to raise their standard of living.

Using What You Learned

▼ **Read and Remember ——— Writing Workshop**

How has Nigeria changed since 1960? Write a paragraph that tells at least three ways Nigeria has changed.

_____

_____

_____

_____

_____

_____

_____

▼ **Think and Apply ——— Fact or Opinion**

A **fact** is a true statement. An **opinion** is a statement that tells what a person thinks.

Fact: Nigeria has more Muslims than Christians.
Opinion: The Muslims are more important than the Christians.

Write **F** next to each fact below. Write **O** next to each opinion. You should find three sentences that are opinions. The first one is done for you.

___F___ 1. Nigeria gets oil from the Gulf of Guinea.

_____ 2. Nigeria earns most of its money by exporting oil.

_____ 3. Southern Nigeria is a better place than northern Nigeria.

_____ 4. Nigeria is using oil money to start heavy industries.

_____ 5. Abuja is in the center of Nigeria.

_____ 6. Abuja is a prettier city than Lagos.

_____ 7. Nigeria is a member of OPEC.

_____ 8. Nigeria has over 250 ethnic groups.

_____ 9. Nigerian farmers grow the best food in Africa.

_____ 10. Nigeria has the largest population in Africa.

▼ Skill Builder —— Reading a Bar Graph

A **bar graph** shows facts by using bars of different lengths. The bar graph on page 58 shows how much money Nigeria earned from exporting oil in 1980, 1985, and 1989. Look at the graph. Then write the answer to each question.

1. What do the numbers at the bottom of the graph stand for?

_____

2. How much money did Nigeria earn in 1980? _____

3. How much money did Nigeria earn in 1985? _____

4. When did Nigeria earn the most money? _____

5. When did Nigeria earn the least money? _____

6. How much more money did Nigeria earn in 1985 than in 1989?

_____

7. Write a sentence that tells how the amount of money Nigeria earned

changed from 1980 to 1989. _____

_____

Chapter Eight

Kenya: A Growing Nation in East Africa

NEW WORDS

altitude

agriculture

cassava

sisal

tourism

Kenya is an African nation that does not have gold, diamonds, or oil. It has no coal, iron, or minerals. This nation has few resources. But Kenya has fertile land and beautiful places to visit. How can Kenyans build a modern nation without resources? You will find the answers in this chapter.

KENYA

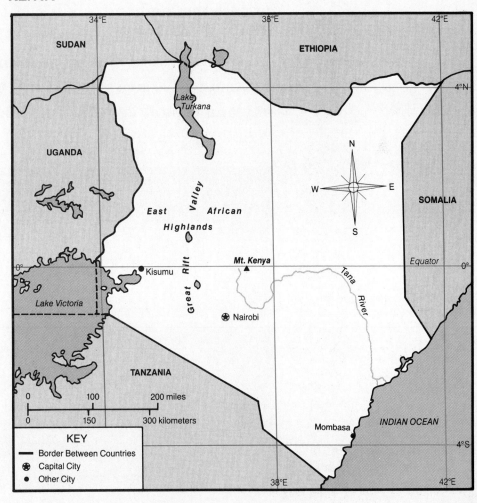

Find Kenya on the map on page 63. Notice that the Equator passes right through the middle of the nation. Also notice that the Indian Ocean is east of Kenya.

There are three important landform regions in this nation. Eastern Kenya has narrow lowlands near the Indian Ocean. There are beautiful beaches near the ocean. The soil in part of this area is fertile and good for farming. Tropical trees grow in this hot, humid region. Kenya's largest port, Mombasa, is on the Indian Ocean.

The largest landform in Kenya is a group of plateaus that covers three fourths of the nation. These plateaus are low near the coast and get higher as you move inland. The plateaus get very little rain. Dry savanna grasslands and deserts cover the plateaus. Nomads raise cattle on the plateaus. Many wild animals also live on the plateaus. Today these animals are protected by laws that say they may not be hunted. Several national parks protect the land and wildlife of the plateau region.

The southwest highlands are Kenya's third landform. This hilly area makes up only one fifth of Kenya's land. But most of Kenya's people live there. Kenya's largest city and capital is in the highlands. It is the city of Nairobi. A small part of Lake Victoria, the largest lake

▶ This man works on a farm in the highlands of Kenya.

◀ Many Kenyans work on plantations that grow cash crops.

in Africa, is in Kenya. The Great Rift Valley is also there. The rainfall and rich soil in this valley make it a good place for farming. Many Kenyans work as farmers in the highlands. The land of the highlands is much higher than the area near the sea coast. This high **altitude** gives this region a cool climate. Kenyans live in the highlands because of the cool, pleasant climate.

Kenyans earn a living in three important ways. The first and most important way is by **agriculture**, or farming. About half of Kenya's farmers grow crops for their own use. Some of these crops are corn, beans, potatoes, and **cassava**. Cassava is a root plant that is like a sweet potato. Some farmers also raise sheep, goats, and cattle. Some farmers sell part of these crops to other Kenyans. Farmers also get income by exporting cash crops. Coffee is the nation's most important cash crop. Kenya earns more money from coffee than from any other product. Kenya also exports tea, nuts, cotton, and **sisal**. Sisal is a plant that is used to make rope.

Cash crops are usually grown on large plantations in the fertile highlands. These plantations were started by the British in the late 1800s when Kenya was a colony.

White plantation owners hired black Kenyans to work for them for little pay. When Kenya became a nation in 1963, the government took over these plantations. The government sold or rented the farms to Africans. Today, most Kenyan farmers own the land they work.

Tourism is a second way Kenyans earn money. Every year thousands of people visit Kenya. Tourists drive through Kenya's national parks. They come to see elephants, zebras, lions, and many other wild animals. Tourists also enjoy beaches near the Indian Ocean. Many Kenyans work in tourist hotels and restaurants.

Kenya is also earning some money from factory goods. Kenya has started new industries with the help of foreign nations. Workers in Mombasa refine oil that has been imported. And Nairobi has factories that make paper, cement, machines, and cloth. Each year many new factories are built. Kenya still imports most of the factory goods it needs from nations in Western Europe.

▶ Nairobi is the capital of Kenya.

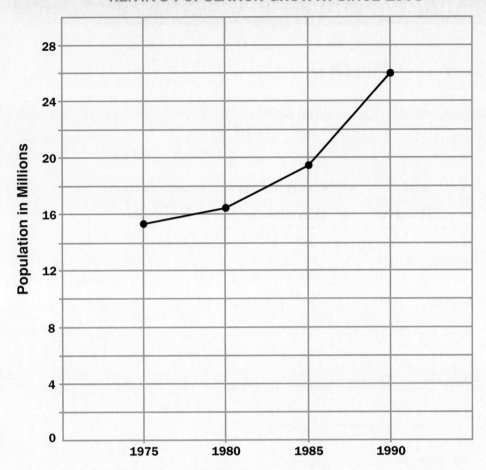

Who are the 26 million people of this nation? About two thirds of them are Christians. Many other Kenyans follow traditional African religions. These African religions believe in one god and many spirits. Some Kenyans are Muslims. Almost all of Kenya's people are blacks. These blacks belong to 40 ethnic groups that speak different languages. The language called Swahili is Kenya's official language.

Kenya has changed since it won its freedom from Great Britain in 1963. Most children today learn to read and write. The nation has few mineral resources, but it earns money from farming, tourism, and factory goods. Now Kenya must try hard to solve the problem of a population that is growing very quickly. When Kenya's population grows more slowly, its people will enjoy a higher standard of living.

▼ Read and Remember —— Finish Up

Choose a word in dark print to finish each sentence. Write the words on the correct blanks.

language	**sisal**	**cash crop**	**tourism**
Lake Victoria	**altitude**	**plateaus**	**Nairobi**

1. Most of Kenya is covered with _____.

2. The southwestern highlands have a cool, pleasant climate because of their high _____.

3. Coffee is Kenya's most important _____.

4. Kenya's largest city is _____.

5. The largest lake in Africa is _____.

6. Kenya exports _____, a plant that is used to make rope.

7. Kenya earns money from agriculture, factory goods, and _____.

8. Swahili is the official _____ of Kenya.

▼ Think and Apply —— Compare and Contrast

Read each sentence below. Does it tell how Kenya and Nigeria are alike? Does it tell how they are different? Write an **A** before the statement if it tells how the two nations are alike. Write a **D** before the statement if it tells how they are different.

_____ 1. It is south of the Sahara.

_____ 2. Most people are blacks.

_____ 3. Most money is earned from cash crops.

_____ 4. Most money is earned by exporting oil.

_____ 5. There are many ethnic groups.

_____ 6. The Great Rift Valley goes through it.

_____ 7. Swahili is the official language.

_____ 8. Tourists watch wildlife in national parks.

_____ 9. It was once a colony.

▼ Skill Builder —— Understanding Line Graphs

Line graphs are used to show **trends**. Trends are changes that take place over a period of time.

The line graph on page 67 shows how Kenya's population has changed since 1975. Look at the line graph. Then finish each sentence in Group A with an answer from Group B. Write the letter of the correct answer on the blank line.

Group A	**Group B**
1. In 1975, Kenya's population was about _____.	a. smaller
2. In 1980, Kenya's population was about _____.	b. grow
3. In 1990, Kenya's population was about _____.	c. 16 and 1/2 million
4. The graph does not show the year 1970. We can guess that Kenya's population in 1970 was _____ than in 1975.	d. 26 million
5. The graph does not show the year 1995. We can guess that Kenya's population will be _____ in 1995.	e. 15 and 1/2 million
6. In Kenya, the trend has been for the population to _____.	f. larger

Chapter Nine

The Republic of South Africa: Africa's Developed Nation

NEW WORDS

suburbs

apartheid

escarpments

racial groups

homelands

It is the end of a busy workday in a South African city. Black workers leave the factories where they have made chemicals, steel, cloth, and food products. And white workers leave the company offices where they have worked at comfortable jobs. Black workers crowd onto buses that take them to an all-black slum. White workers drive their cars to all-white **suburbs**. These suburbs are neighborhoods outside the busy city. In the past, South African laws kept blacks and whites apart almost everywhere. These laws were part of a system called **apartheid**. In this chapter, you will learn about the land, people, and laws in South Africa.

▶ Many people worked to stop apartheid in South Africa.

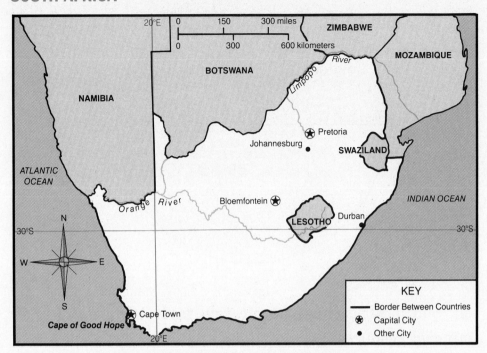

The Republic of South Africa is the only developed nation on the continent of Africa. Find South Africa on the map above. Notice that South Africa has several harbors on its coasts. The Indian Ocean is to the east of South Africa, and the Atlantic Ocean is to the west.

South Africa has four important landforms. There are narrow lowlands on the east coast. Mountains rise above the coast at the southern tip of the nation. Plateaus cover many other parts of the nation. Sharp cliffs called **escarpments** form the edge of the plateau.

Most of the nation has a mild climate because it is far from the Equator. Many parts of the coastal lowlands have hot, humid summers and dry winters. The high altitude of the plateau gives it a cooler climate. Most of South Africa does not get enough rain. The western part of the nation is so dry that it has two large deserts.

South Africa's rich minerals have helped the nation become developed. South Africa has more diamonds and gold than any other nation in the world. And South Africa has almost every other resource it needs, except

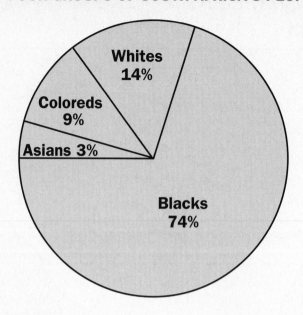

oil. South Africa has become rich from using its mineral resources.

South Africa exports some of its minerals. South Africa also uses its minerals to make factory goods. South Africa is an industrial nation with many kinds of factories. South African factories make almost every product the nation needs. These factories manufacture clothing, machines, cars, tools, and many other products.

Today about 36 million people live in South Africa. Apartheid laws separated people into four **racial groups**. Blacks are the largest racial group and make up about three fourths of the population. Whites make up about one seventh of the population. Their families came from the Netherlands and Great Britain many years ago. Coloreds, or people of mixed races, are the third group. Coloreds may come from white and black or white and Asian families. Indians from Asia are the smallest racial group in South Africa.

The white people of South Africa made apartheid laws to keep the four racial groups apart. These laws separated whites from other races at work, in schools, and in neighborhoods. The racial groups were not treated equally. Whites still have most of the power and a high standard of living. Whites control mines, businesses, factories, and government. White South Africans have large, modern farms and ranches that produce many kinds of cash crops. People of other races often work on these farms, raising fruit, grains, tobacco, and sheep. Coloreds and Indians have less power than whites.

Blacks have the smallest amount of power. The white government forced many blacks to move to ten **homelands**. These homelands are small, separate areas inside South Africa. Homelands have few modern services and a lot of poverty. These crowded homelands cover a small part of the nation's land, but three fourths of the nation's people live there. Blacks may vote for leaders in their separate homelands. But blacks may not vote for leaders of South Africa, even though blacks make up most of the population.

It is hard to earn a living in these homelands. There are few minerals in the homelands. There are few factory or government jobs. Most people in the homelands are subsistence farmers. But the soil is not fertile, and farmers do not have modern tools.

People all over the world worked to end the apartheid system. Many nations did not buy goods made in South

◄ Many black people in South Africa live in neighborhoods like this one.

▲ These South Africans are building a home.

Africa because they thought apartheid was wrong. Other nations stopped selling goods to South Africa.

South Africa finally ended some of the apartheid laws. In 1990, the government let Nelson Mandela out of jail. Mandela is a black South African leader. He was in jail for 27 years because he spoke out against apartheid. Today the laws allow hotels, restaurants, and movie theaters to serve all races. People of different races are now allowed to marry one another.

In 1992, a special whites-only election was held. White South Africans voted to support the white government's plans to end apartheid. White leaders met with Mandela to plan a new kind of government. Black Africans will have more power in the government. But the changes will not be easy. Some white people still refuse to allow black people equal rights. Some black groups do not want Mandela and his followers to gain power.

Meanwhile, the white-run government began spending more on housing, schools, and hospitals for black people. Watch the news for other changes in South Africa.

Using What You Learned

▼ **Read and Remember —— True or False**

Write **T** next to each sentence that is true. Write **F** next to each sentence that is false. There are three false sentences. On the lines below, rewrite the false sentences to make them true.

_____ 1. South Africa is a developing nation.

_____ 2. An escarpment is a cliff at the edge of a plateau.

_____ 3. South Africa is near the Equator and very hot.

_____ 4. Apartheid laws kept the racial groups apart.

_____ 5. Long ago, white people came from the Netherlands and Great Britain to South Africa.

_____ 6. Apartheid laws were fair to blacks.

_____ 7. South Africa has many minerals.

_____ 8. Nelson Mandela is a black South African leader.

_____

_____

_____

▼ **Skill Builder —— Understanding Pie Graphs**

A **pie graph** is a circle that has been divided into parts. Each part looks like a piece of pie. All the parts make up the whole circle.

The pie graph on page 72 shows how the people of South Africa were divided into four racial groups under apartheid laws. The four groups make up the whole population of South Africa.

Look at the pie graph on page 72 again. Then use the answers in dark print to finish each sentence. Write the answers you choose on the correct blanks.

Blacks   Asians   74%   14%   9%   3%

1. The blacks are _____ of South Africa's population.

2. The whites are _____ of the population.

3. _____ of the people are Asians.

4. The Coloreds are _____ of the population.

5. _____ are the largest group.

6. _____ are the smallest group.

▼ Think and Apply —— Categories

Read the words in each group. Decide how they are alike. Find the best title in the box for each group. Write the title on the line above each group.

Blacks in South Africa	**Developed Nation**	**Minerals**
Whites in South Africa	**Racial Groups**	**Landforms**

1. _____

   control the mines
   control the factories
   government leaders

2. _____

   diamonds
   gold
   copper

3. _____

   escarpments
   plateaus
   lowlands

4. _____

   Asians
   blacks
   Coloreds

5. _____

   many large cities
   many factories
   modern farms

6. _____

   largest racial group
   were forced to live in
      homelands
   were not allowed to vote

Chapter Ten

Working for a Better Africa

NEW WORDS

hunger
desertification
famine
illiterate
education
foreign aid
experts

An African family is planting cassava on its small farm. For many years, the family has not grown enough food for their seven children. This year, the family is planting a new kind of seed that grows more cassava. This one small change could help this family a lot. If they grow more food than they need, the family can sell the extra cassava. With the cash they get, the family can buy tools or fertilizers. Then they could grow even more cassava next year. Changing the way people farm is one way Africans are ending poverty.

Africans have a hard time ending poverty because millions of people are hungry. When people are hungry, getting food is the most important thing to them. Hungry people get tired easily. So they may not have the energy to plant more seeds or water their crops.

▶ These Africans are working to grow corn.

▲ Most children in Africa today are learning to read and write.

When people are hungry, they do not have energy to go to school to learn new ways of farming. **Hunger** is a problem that must be solved before any other problems can be solved.

Africa's rapid population growth makes it hard to solve the problem of hunger. The number of people to feed keeps getting larger. The population is getting larger because most families have many children. The population is also growing because Africans are getting better health care. So people are living longer than they did 50 years ago. Governments are teaching people to have fewer children. But many Africans want large families to help with the farm work.

It is hard to grow enough food for all of these people. In many places the soil is poor, farms are small, and there is little water. Insects often destroy crops in the fields. Most farmers use simple, traditional hand tools and farm the same land year after year without using fertilizers.

Sometimes changes in the climate make it hard to farm or keep herds of animals. In some places, such as the Sahel, grasslands are getting smaller and deserts are growing larger. This is called **desertification**. There is less land for raising food because of desertification.

There are three reasons why African deserts are growing larger. First, some areas have droughts that last for years. Since there is little or no rain, plants and trees die and the desert grows larger. Second, in some places, people have chopped down too many trees. Without trees, the soil erodes and fertile land turns into desert. Third, nomads' hungry sheep and cattle sometimes eat grass down to the roots. When the grass is gone, wind blows away the soil. In a time with little rain, this land without grass becomes a desert.

Africans are trying to stop desertification. In nations such as Kenya, people have planted millions of new trees and plants. Trees stop the soil from eroding. Some nations are also teaching nomads how to save the grasslands.

Famine has been another problem in many African nations. During a famine, many people are so hungry that they starve to death. Since the 1960s, there have been terrible famines in several African nations. Most famines happened because of wars, desertification, and droughts. Africans have been so hungry that they have

◀ Cattle help cause desertification in Africa.

79

THREE AFRICAN COUNTRIES SOUTH OF THE SAHARA				
Country	Population	Natural Resources	Important Exports	Official Language(s)
Nigeria	120 million	oil, coal iron, tin	oil, coal, palm oil	English
Kenya	26 million	trees, wildlife, fertile soil in the highlands	coffee, tea, refined oil	English Swahili
South Africa	41 million	gold, tin, diamonds, coal, iron, uranium	diamonds, gold, metals, food	English, Afrikaans

eaten seeds that should have been planted. So no new crops could grow, and even more people starved. People from many nations have sent food to Africa. But it is hard to get the food to people in faraway villages.

Africans are trying to stop hunger. Many Africans use better seeds to grow more crops. And Africans use chemicals to kill insects. But these solutions can cause more problems. Some of the chemicals that kill insects can hurt people who eat the food. To use chemicals safely, farmers need to learn more about them.

Many Africans are **illiterate**. This means that they do not know how to read or write. In Mali, about two people out of twenty can read the directions on a bag of fertilizer. For hundreds of years, Africans did not need to know how to read in order to farm and live. Many Africans today need a better **education** in order to have a higher standard of living. So governments are building new schools and training teachers. In Kenya, most children now go to school. Half the adults have learned to read.

When they can read and write, Africans will be better able to work in factories. As nations get more industries, they will get stronger. And Africans will have a better chance to earn a higher standard of living.

Foreign aid is helping African nations. Foreign aid is money and help that one nation gives another. Japan, the United States, France, and other nations give aid to Africa. African nations use foreign aid to build dams, roads, industries, and schools. Some nations send **experts** to teach people new ways to farm and use resources. But many Africans do not want foreign aid. Most nations that give aid make Africans buy goods from them. Sometimes the aid is in the form of loans. Then Africans must pay back the money. Others say that aid pays for roads and buildings but does not help the people who really need it.

Today, Africa's people are working to solve many hard problems. Most nations in Africa have been independent for only about 30 years. These young African nations are trying to become nations where all people can have a high standard of living.

▼ This is a classroom in Kenya.

Using What You Learned

▼ Read and Remember —— Find the Answer

Put a check (✔) next to each sentence below that tells about problems in Africa. You should check five sentences.

_____ 1. Millions of people do not know how to read.

_____ 2. The deserts are growing larger.

_____ 3. There are too many large cities.

_____ 4. The population is growing very fast.

_____ 5. Millions of people are hungry.

_____ 6. There is a lot of air pollution.

_____ 7. Millions of people are very poor.

_____ 8. There are too many factories.

▼ Think and Apply —— Analogies

Use a word in dark print to finish each sentence.

desertification **Sahara** **oil**
illiterate **poverty**

1. Not enough rain is to drought as not enough money is to _____.

2. Foreign aid is to poverty as planting new trees is to _____.

3. Large families are to rapid population growth as not enough schools are to _____ people.

4. Diamonds are to South Africa as _____ is to Nigeria.

5. The Sahel is to grasslands as the _____ is to deserts.

Tables are used to learn facts quickly. Read the table on page 80 to learn facts about Kenya, Nigeria, and South Africa. Then write the answer to each question.

1. What are Kenya's natural resources?

_____

2. What is Kenya's official language?

_____

3. What does Nigeria export?

_____

4. What is Nigeria's population?

_____

5. What are South Africa's natural resources?

_____

6. What does South Africa export?

_____

7. Which country has two official languages?

_____

8. Which country has the largest population?

_____

Tourists and Hunters in Kenya

It is evening in the African savanna, and hundreds of wild animals gather around water. Elephants, water buffalo, giraffes, deer, and other wildlife come to drink.

Tourists from around the world watch the animals. The tourists are in a hotel built in the top of a huge tree. They have come to see one of the world's great sights—the wild animals of Africa.

But unless something is done soon, the animals might be found only in zoos. There may be no wildlife in the savanna for the tourists to watch. Africans are shooting the animals by the thousands. They are selling the animals' skins and horns to earn money. Then goods made of the skins and horns are sold to people around the world.

Location/Place

Kenya is on the eastern side of Africa. Kenya has some of the world's most beautiful land. A large number of the world's wild animals live here.

Kenya's land goes from the coast along the Indian Ocean to mountains covered with snow. There visitors enjoy snowball fights near the Equator.

Human/Environment Interaction

The land and animals make Kenya a special place for tourists. More than 10 percent of the country's land is in national parks. Thousands of tourists visit these parks each year. These tourists spend hundreds of millions of dollars on hotels, food, and other needs. This money is badly needed in Kenya.

But some people in Kenya and nearby countries want to make money in a way that hurts tourism. These people kill elephants for their tusks

KENYA

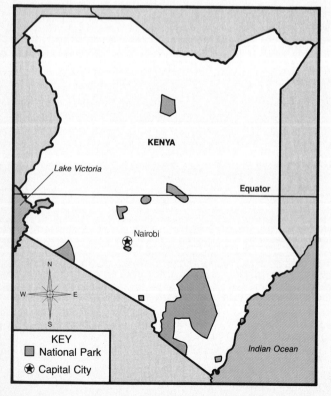

84

and other animals for their skins. In only ten years, almost 50,000 elephants were killed in Kenya.

If the killing is not stopped, more than animals will die. Tourism will die, too.

Movement

The people of Africa are not the only ones to blame for the killing of the animals. People in many parts of the world want goods made of horns or animal skins.

Kenya is trying to stop the killing. But the parks are very large, and the hunters hide themselves well. And as long as there are people who want to buy these things, there will be hunters to kill the wildlife in Kenya's parks.

▲ Many tourists come to Kenya to see the wildlife.

Write About It

It is your job to convince people to stop killing the wildlife in Kenya's parks. What arguments and facts can you use to win people over? Write a paragraph telling what you would say to these people.

_____

_____

_____

_____

_____

_____

UNIT 3

South and Southeast Asia

Dear Grandpa,

It's been raining since we got here. I'm starting to get used to it though. Most of the cities are on the coast or near rivers. Lots of people use boats and bicycles to get around.

Love, Vanessa

Julian King
1920 Central Avenue
Houston, Texas
U.S.A. 77089

REPUBLIK INDONESIA 275.

REPUBLIK INDONESIA

REPUBLIK INDONESIA

SINGAPORE

87

Chapter Eleven

Getting to Know South and Southeast Asia

NEW WORDS

seasonal wind

monsoon

slash and burn agriculture

wet rice farming

terraces

commercial agriculture

cottage industries

South and Southeast Asia are two parts of one large region. South Asia includes the nation of India, which is a large peninsula. It also includes nations surrounding India to the northwest, the north, the east, and the island nation just south of India. Southeast Asia includes the nations east of India and south of China, and the nations between the Indian and Pacific oceans. Find South and Southeast Asia on the map on page 89. This region is the most populated region in the world. More than one and a half billion people live here. In this

▶ The Himalaya are the world's tallest mountains.

chapter, you will learn more about the land and people in this crowded region.

Most of South and Southeast Asia is covered with plains and plateaus. There are narrow lowlands near the coasts. The tallest mountains in the world, the Himalaya, are in the northern part of South Asia. The highest of these mountains is Mt. Everest. It is almost six miles higher than the land on the coast of Asia. The Himalaya form a wall that separates South Asia from northern Asia. So the mountains make it hard for people to trade with other people in Asia. Many different cultures developed in this region because people could not share ideas easily. The mountains are important because many rivers start out in these high mountains. These rivers have helped people to have land and water for farming.

SOUTH AND SOUTHEAST ASIA

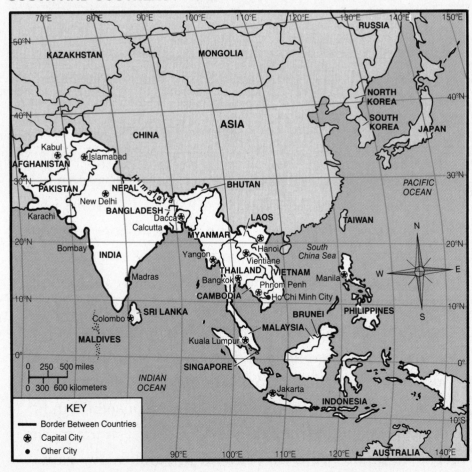

▲ Most people in South and Southeast Asia live near rivers.

For 5000 years, people have lived close to the long rivers of South and Southeast Asia. They have farmed the fertile soil in these river valleys. The valleys receive fertile silt from floods that come almost every year. People use river water for irrigation. Asians also travel on the rivers in small boats. The Mekong River in Southeast Asia and the Ganges River in India are two of the most important rivers in the region. There are also other long rivers. Many people live in the river valleys.

The climate of South and Southeast Asia is special in two ways. First, the region is near the Equator. So nations in this region have hot, tropical climates. Second, this area has a **seasonal wind** called a **monsoon**. A monsoon always blows from one direction during a season of the year. In the winter, the monsoon winds bring cold, dry air from the north. In the summer, the monsoon winds bring hot, humid air and heavy rains from the sea in the south. Areas near the coast get the heaviest rains. Parts of India and Pakistan that are far from the coast and the monsoons have a dry, desert climate.

Most people in South and Southeast Asia are farmers. These farmers use three different kinds of agriculture. First, farmers in mountain areas with heavy forests use **slash-and-burn agriculture**. Farmers chop down trees in the forest and then burn them. The ashes from the burned trees make the soil fertile. The farmers grow crops for a few years, until the soil is no longer fertile. Then farmers move to another part of the forest and chop down more trees. This kind of farming works best where there is a lot of unused land and few people. These farmers have destroyed many forests in Asia.

The second kind of agriculture is called **wet rice farming**. Rice grows well in this region's hot, wet climate. Rice farming works best in places where there is plenty of water. This kind of farming also needs many

◄ Many farmers in South and Southeast Asia grow rice on terraces.

91

people to do the work. Rice seeds are first planted in small fields. Later, workers move the small rice plants to another field with a lot of water. In hilly parts of South and Southeast Asia, farmers have built flat fields into hillsides. These flat **terraces** have dirt walls to keep water in the fields. The tropical climate makes this region good for wet rice farming. And the large number of workers also makes wet rice farming a good way to grow food for this region.

The third kind of farming is **commercial agriculture**. In this kind of farming, people grow cash crops on plantations. Many plantations started in the 1800s when this region was ruled by European nations. Some Europeans came to Asia to start farms so they could send the crops back to Europe and make money. Rubber, tea, cotton, and sugar cane were, and still are, some of the region's most important cash crops.

Fertile soil is one of the region's most important resources. Plant products such as lumber, spices, tea, and bamboo, are important exports. About half of the world's tin is mined in Southeast Asia. Some nations have a few other minerals. And fishing is important in some coastal areas.

▶ Commercial agriculture is important to South and Southeast Asia.

◀ Making umbrellas is an important cottage industry in this Asian village.

Most nations in this region were once colonies of European nations. These nations built few factories in the region. Europeans wanted to sell the factory goods made in Europe to Asians. So Europeans did not want Asia to have its own factories. Instead, Europeans wanted Asians to grow crops that could be sold in Europe. So Europeans started plantations and grew cash crops. They built roads to connect plantations with ports on the coasts. Europeans only built factories to get crops ready for shipping.

Many factories are being built in the region. India has steel, cement, and fertilizer factories. Singapore is known for its shipbuilding, **electronic** goods, and oil-refining industries. Malaysia has new computer factories. Modern industries are changing traditional ways of life. But most industries are still small **cottage industries**. In cottage industries, people produce small goods, such as shirts or pillows, in their own homes. These workers use simple machines to make things they can sell.

Many different ethnic groups live in South and Southeast Asia. These ethnic groups have different languages, religions, and standards of living. In the next chapters, you will learn about people who live in three nations in this crowded region.

Using What You Learned

Write **T** next to each sentence that is true. Write **F** next to each sentence that is false. There are three false sentences.

_____ 1. Monsoon winds bring lots of rain in the summer.

_____ 2. The Himalaya are low mountains.

_____ 3. For thousands of years, people in the region lived near rivers.

_____ 4. Floods destroy the region's fertile farmlands.

_____ 5. Many nations in the region have a cold climate.

_____ 6. People who do slash-and-burn agriculture chop down forest trees to plant crops.

_____ 7. South and Southeast Asia has a huge population.

▼ Think and Apply —— Finding the Main Idea

Read each group of sentences below. One of the sentences is a main idea. Two sentences support the main idea. Write an **M** next to the sentence that is the main idea in each group.

1. _____ a. Monsoons blow in one direction in the winter.

   _____ b. Monsoons blow in another direction in the summer.

   _____ c. Monsoons are seasonal winds.

2. _____ a. Some farmers use slash-and-burn agriculture or wet rice farming.

   _____ b. Farmers use three kinds of agriculture.

   _____ c. Some farmers grow cash crops.

3. _____ a. There are peninsulas and plateaus.

   _____ b. There are many landforms in South and Southeast Asia.

   _____ c. There are lowlands and tall mountains.

4. _____ a. Cash crops are sold to other nations.

_____ b. South and Southeast Asia earns money from commercial agriculture.

_____ c. Rubber, tea, and sugar cane are some of the region's cash crops.

▼ Skill Builder —— Reviewing Latitude and Longitude

Lines of latitude are imaginary lines. They run east and west around Earth. Lines of longitude are imaginary lines, too. They run north and south around Earth. Lines of longitude meet at the North and South poles.

Latitude and longitude are measured in degrees. The Equator is an important line of latitude. It is at 0° latitude. The most important line of longitude is the Prime Meridian. The Prime Meridian is at 0° longitude.

Lines of latitude and longitude form grids on maps. These grids help us find places on the maps. We can use lines of latitude and longitude to find places on the map of South and Southeast Asia. Madras is a city in India. It has a latitude of 13°N and a longitude of 80°E. This means Madras is 13 degrees north of the Equator and 80 degrees east of the Prime Meridian.

Look at the map of South and Southeast Asia on page 89. Then finish each sentence in Group A with an answer from Group B. Write the letter of the correct answer on the blank line.

Group A	**Group B**
1. The Equator is a line of _____.	a. 2°N
2. The Prime Meridian is at _____.	b. 107°E
3. The latitude of Singapore is _____.	c. latitude
4. The longitude of Jakarta is _____.	d. New Delhi
5. The city of _____ has a latitude and longitude of 28°N, 77°E.	e. 0° longitude

Chapter Twelve

India: A Changing Nation of Villages and Cities

NEW WORDS

ancestors
Hinduism
caste
priests

▼ Nearly three fourths of all Indians live in villages.

In many parts of India, village people live the way their **ancestors** did. Just as women in their families did hundreds of years ago, women today start each day by walking to a well. There they fill jars with water. The women carry the jars on their heads to their small homes.

About 70 percent of Indians are still rural farmers. They live in small villages. Many people grow crops on the same land and in the same way that their ancestors did. Farmers still plant and pick beans, grains, and vegetables by hand. Some farmers keep cattle and water buffaloes to plow fields. This traditional life is important to Indians. In this chapter, you will study the history,

land, and people of this changing nation of villages.

Find India on the map below. Notice that the Indian Ocean is to the south of India. There are narrow lowland plains along the coasts. Two large port cities, Madras and Calcutta, are on the plains. There are also many small fishing villages there. The coastal plain is along the edge of southern India. Southern India is a large peninsula. The Deccan Plateau covers most of the land on India's peninsula. People farm, raise animals, and mine minerals on the Deccan Plateau.

North of this plateau is the Northern Plain. India's longest and most important rivers are in this plain. The Ganges River is the longest river in India. It starts in

INDIA

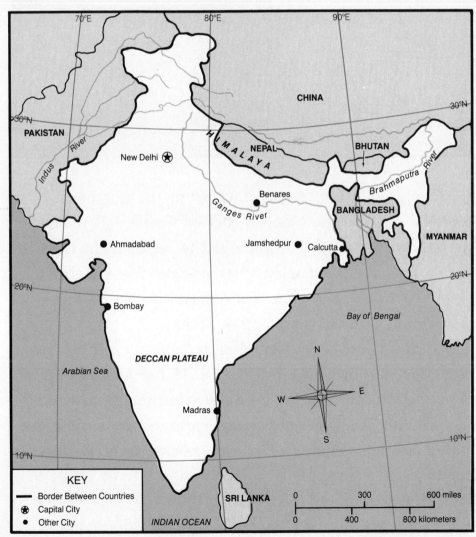

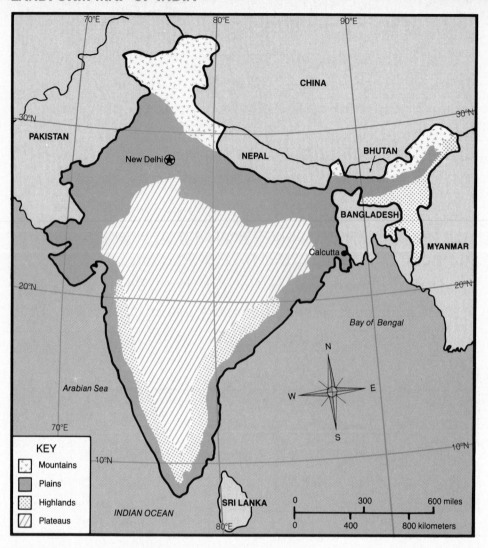

the Himalaya Mountains, which form the northern border of India. The Ganges carries fertile soil to the plains. So this area has some of the best soil in the world. This flat land is easy to irrigate. Most of India's people live in this region. The capital of the nation, New Delhi, is near the Ganges River.

In India, there are three climate seasons during the year. The nation has a cool season, a hot season, and a rainy season. During the rainy season, monsoon winds blow humid air from the Indian Ocean into south India. Indian farmers depend on the monsoons to grow food. But in some years, monsoons come too late or bring too little rain to produce crops. Sometimes it rains so much that crops are ruined. But the monsoon rains usually help Indians grow enough food to feed their people.

India today is a developing nation with a huge population. China is the only nation in the world with more people than India. More than 844 million people live in India. The population is growing very fast.

India was a colony ruled by Great Britain for over 100 years. The British started plantations to grow cash crops, such as tea, tobacco, and cotton. But these are not food crops. And people could not grow food crops, such as rice and wheat, on land that was planted with these cash crops. So many of India's people went hungry.

Indians thought the British were unfair, so they worked to make India free. By 1947, India controlled its own government. Since then, the government has been working to end hunger. The government lends money to farmers so they can use modern ways of farming. Farmers use these loans to buy fertilizer, new kinds of seeds, and irrigation systems.

Other ways of life in India have changed since 1947. When India was a colony, it sent most of its raw materials to factories in Great Britain. But today, more of these resources stay inside the nation. India has started many factories since 1947. These factories use Indian workers and resources to make steel, cloth,

◀ New irrigation systems help Indian farmers grow more food.

▶ India's cities are very crowded.

cement, and many machines and tools. India is a very important industrial nation.

Many Indians have left villages to work in cities. Two of the largest cities are Calcutta and Bombay. Both of these are important port cities.

Most Indians follow the Hindu religion. **Hinduism** gives hope to many people with a low standard of living. Hindus believe that every person has a soul that never dies. Hindus believe that if a person lives a good life, the soul will have a better life the next time it is born. Hindus try to do good things so they will be reborn into a higher **caste**. A caste is a group that gives people certain jobs and rules for living. The Hindu **priests**, or leaders of the religion, are in the highest caste. Below the priests are store owners, farmers, workers, and servants. Some people with the lowest standard of living do not belong to any caste.

India has changed a lot since it became a nation in 1947. The nation now has many industries. It grows more food for its people. In the years ahead, many more changes will be needed to help India become part of the modern, developed world.

Using What You Learned

▼ Read and Remember —— Finish Up

Choose a word in dark print to finish up each sentence. Write the words on the correct blanks.

Deccan Plateau	**ancestors**	**villages**	**Hindu**
government	**monsoon**	**Ganges River**	**caste**

1. Many Indians live today just as their _____ did.

2. Most Indians live in small _____.

3. The _____ is south of the Northern Plain and has many minerals.

4. The city of New Delhi is close to the _____.

5. Indian farmers need the summer _____ rains to grow food.

6. The _____ has helped farmers grow more food.

7. Most Indians believe in the _____ religion.

8. Hindu priests belong in the highest _____.

▼ Skill Builder —— Reviewing Landform Maps

You learned that landform maps help you find out about the landforms of a region. Landform maps show where there are plains, plateaus, and mountains. The map of India on page 98 shows the different landforms in that nation.

Look at the landform map of India on page 98. Then write **T** next to each sentence that is true. Write **F** next to each sentence that is false.

_____ 1. India has mountains in the north.

_____ 2. There are plains on the west coast.

_____ 3. There are mountains in the south of India.

101

_____ 4. There are mountains near China.

_____ 5. There are highlands in the west of India.

_____ 6. New Delhi and Calcutta are in the plains.

_____ 7. Central India has a plateau.

_____ 8. There are plateaus in the far east of India.

▼ Think and Apply —— Cause and Effect

Match each cause on the left with an effect on the right. Write the letter of the effect on the correct blank.

Cause

1. The Northern Plain is very fertile, so _____.

2. Heavy rains cause floods on the Ganges River, so _____.

3. India now has many factories, so _____.

4. Indians thought the British were unfair, so _____.

5. Hindus want to be reborn into a higher caste, so _____.

6. The government lends money to farmers, so _____.

Effect

a. the nation makes cloth, machines, and cement.

b. Indians worked to make India a free nation.

c. they try to do good things.

d. thousands of farms and villages are on the plain.

e. land near the river gets fertile soil from floods.

f. farmers are able to buy fertilizers and new kinds of seeds.

Chapter Thirteen

Thailand: The Rice Bowl of Southeast Asia

NEW WORDS

teak
invested
Buddhists
temples

Small plants fill the wet fields of central Thailand. Dirt dams one or two feet high hold water in the fields. Workers bend over the plants in the fields. They are pushing young green rice plants into soft mud. In a few weeks, the fields will look like a huge green lake. As the plants get older, the grains of rice turn yellowish-white.

THAILAND

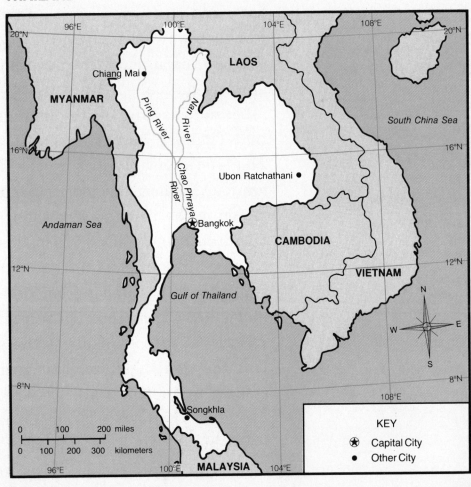

▶ These farmers are working in a rice field in Thailand.

These fields grow rice, the most important crop in Thailand. Many people in this Southeast Asian nation eat rice three times a day. And Thais make sandals, hats, and roofs out of rice straw. Thailand exports more rice than any other nation in the world. In this chapter, you will learn about the land and people in this rice-growing nation.

Locate Thailand on the map on page 103. Notice that Thailand has borders with four nations. Most of Thailand's long coast is on the Gulf of Thailand. There are four landform regions in Thailand. The first landform region is the peninsula in the south. This region has mountains and rolling hills. This southern peninsula is covered with tropical forests and jungles. Not much rice is grown here. Rubber from rubber trees and tin from mines are the main exports from this region.

North of the peninsula is the second landform region. It is the Central Plain. This region has a warm, wet climate and fertile soil. It is the largest rice-producing region in Thailand. The important Chao Phraya River is in this region. This long river begins in Thailand's northern mountains and flows to the Gulf of Thailand.

Like other rivers in South and Southeast Asia, the Chao Phraya has floods which bring silt to the river valley. During the dry months, farmers use river water to irrigate their fields. The Chao Phraya is also used for transportation. People use this waterway to send crops to different parts of Thailand.

The third landform region in Thailand is the Northeast Plateau. This area is the most populated region in Thailand. People irrigate the plateau with water from three nearby rivers. A lot of rice is grown on this plateau.

The fourth landform region is the Northern Mountains. Thick forests cover these mountains. Many streams flow through this area. There are fertile valleys around these streams. Farmers grow rice in the narrow mountain valleys. People cut **teak** trees from the forests of this region. Then they export the lumber.

The climate of Thailand has helped the nation become a large producer of rice and other crops. Thailand has a

◀ The Chao Phraya River is very important to Thailand.

warm tropical climate. Monsoon winds bring heavy rains from July to December. Rice and other tropical food crops grow well in this wet, tropical climate.

Bangkok is the largest city in Thailand. It is also the capital city. Bangkok is on the Chao Phraya River. Find Bangkok on the map on page 103. Rice farmers use the Chao Phraya to send their crops to Bangkok to be exported to other nations. So Bangkok is also an important port city.

Only a small number of Thailand's people work in industries. But Thailand now earns more than one third of its money from mining and manufacturing. Foreign businesses have **invested** money in factories in the Bangkok area. These foreign businesses use their money to open new Thai factories. Workers manufacture cars, computers, paper, and machines. Thailand also earns money from its tourist industry. Tourists come to use the beaches, listen to Thai music, and watch Thai dances.

Most Thais are **Buddhists**. Buddhists believe in the teachings of a religious leader named Buddha. Buddha lived about 2500 years ago. He taught people to be kind, peaceful, and helpful. Buddha taught that people can only be happy if they forget about money and things.

▶ This Buddhist temple is in Bangkok.

◀ These Thai students are in a class.

Many statues of Buddha show him sitting quietly and praying. Buddhists have **temples** in most Thai villages. People in the villages have fairs and holiday parties at these temples. Buddha's birthday is a holiday all over the nation.

The name Thailand means "Land of the Free." Thailand has always ruled itself. It has never been a colony. This nation now has about 56 million people. They speak the Thai language.

Thailand is a developing nation where most people are rice farmers in villages. Thais have an average income of about $800 a year. Most Thais live traditional lives. There is enough food for everyone. Cottage industries make beautiful cloth and jewelry. Modern factories build cars and computers. Thailand has a higher standard of living than most nations in South and Southeast Asia. Most people can read and write. Thailand has better roads and railroads than most nations in the region. Farmers are learning modern ways to grow larger crops. The people of Thailand are working hard to export larger farm crops in the years to come.

Using What You Learned

▼ **Read and Remember** —— **Finish the Story**

Bangkok	tropical	colony	teak
monsoon	rubber	rice	free

Thailand has a _____ climate. The _____ winds bring rain

from July to December. The climate and fertile soil help Thailand export

more _____ than any other nation. Thailand also exports

_____ and _____. Most people live in villages, but the nation

has a large capital called _____. Thailand has always been a

_____ nation. It has never been a _____ of a European nation.

▼ **Skill Builder** —— **Using a Distance Scale**

Distance scales help us find distances between places on maps. On the
map of Thailand on page 103, one inch is about 200 miles. To use a distance
scale, you must multiply the number of inches between two places by the
number of miles on the scale. Two inches would be 400 miles on this map.

Choose an answer in dark print to finish each sentence.

3 1/2   400   1 1/2   700   300   2

1. There are about _____ inches between Chiang Mai and Ubon Ratchathani.

2. The distance between Chiang Mai and Ubon Ratchathani is about
   _____ inches.

3. There are about _____ inches between Bangkok and Chiang Mai.

4. The distance between Bangkok and Chiang Mai is about _____ miles.

5. There are about _____ inches between Chiang Mai and Songkhla.

6. The distance between Chiang Mai and Songkhla is about _____ miles.

▼ Think and Apply —— Drawing Conclusions

Read each pair of sentences. Then look in the box for the conclusion you can make. Write the letter of the conclusion on the blank.

1. Rice is grown on the Central Plain, in the Northern Mountains, and on the Northeast Plateau.
   The Southern Peninsula is not a good place to grow rice.

   Conclusion _____

2. Farmers use water from the Chao Phraya River to irrigate their fields.
   Farmers use the Chao Phraya River to ship their crops from their villages to Bangkok.

   Conclusion _____

3. Many tourists visit the cities and beaches of Thailand.
   Tourists enjoy the music and dances of Thailand.

   Conclusion _____

4. There are Buddhist temples in most villages and cities.
   Buddha's birthday is a holiday all over Thailand.

   Conclusion _____

5. Thailand has better transportation than most nations in South and Southeast Asia.
   There is plenty of food for the people of Thailand.

   Conclusion _____

---

a. The Buddhist religion is important in Thailand.

b. Thailand has a higher standard of living than many nations in South and Southeast Asia.

c. Farmers grow rice in many parts of Thailand.

d. Thailand earns money from its tourist industry.

e. The Chao Phraya River is important to the farmers of Thailand.

Chapter Fourteen

Indonesia: One Nation on Thousands of Islands

NEW WORDS

archipelago
erupt
lava
volcanic ash
communication

If you visited Indonesia, you would have a hard time seeing the whole nation. Indonesia has more than 13,600 islands. They are spread out over 3,000 miles in the Indian and Pacific oceans. But even if you visited just a few of these islands, you would notice that Indonesia is a nation of contrasts. You would see farms, oil fields, tin mines, and huge, crowded cities on different islands. Other islands do not have any people living on them. You would see people from over 200 ethnic groups living in different ways. Being spread out over thousands of islands has made it hard for Indonesia to become a nation. As you read this chapter, find out why it has been hard for these islands to form one nation.

▶ Oil is found in some parts of Indonesia.

Find Indonesia on the map below. Notice that the many islands have different sizes and shapes. Borneo and Sumatra are large islands. But some islands are so small that they cannot be shown on your map, even as small dots. All of these islands form a chain of islands called an **archipelago**.

Indonesia has a population of about 188 million people. More than half of the nation's people live on the island of Java. There, almost 2,000 people live in every square mile.

Java is the most important island of Indonesia. The nation's capital, Jakarta, is on Java. Jakarta is a crowded city of about 9 million people. Most of the nation's other large cities are also on Java. Most of the nation's industries are on Java. Many farmers plant crops on the island's fertile soil. The government has tried to make people move to other islands that have fewer people. But people do not want to leave Java.

The coastal plains of Indonesia have some of the nation's best farmland. Farmers grow sugar cane, rice, and rubber in the fertile soil of these plains. The islands

INDONESIA

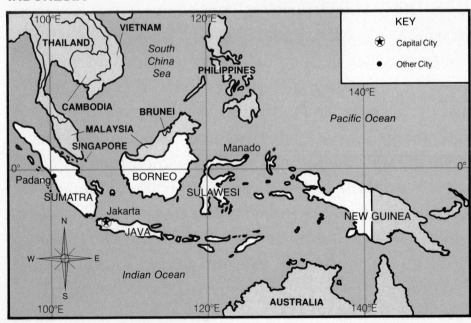

▲ This volcano is on the island of Java in Indonesia.

of Indonesia are also covered with hills and mountains. About 60 mountains are active volcanoes that sometimes **erupt**. When volcanoes erupt, they shoot out hot liquid rocks called **lava** and thick dust called **volcanic ash**. Volcanic ash makes the soil around the volcanoes fertile.

The islands of Indonesia are on or near the Equator. The climate is hot and tropical. Some islands have a lot of rain during the year. Many tropical rain forests grow there. Other islands, such as Java, have a dry monsoon season.

Indonesia has been a trading center for hundreds of years. In the 1500s, traders first came from European nations, such as Great Britain, Portugal, and the Netherlands. These traders wanted to buy spices, such as pepper and cloves, which are grown on these islands. These Europeans called Indonesia the "Spice Islands" because of the plants the islanders grew.

In the 1600s, the Dutch traders, from the Netherlands, decided to take over and rule the islands so that they alone could grow and export spices. The Dutch took some land by fighting and were given some of the land by island rulers. In the mid-1800s, the Dutch started plantations to grow coffee and other crops. Many Dutch people got rich, but they did not share their money with the island people. Indonesians tried to make the Dutch leave for almost 100 years. In 1949, after years of fighting, the Dutch gave Indonesia its freedom.

For many years, it was hard for the many islands to form one nation. There was not much **communication** among the islands. People on different islands did not trade or share ideas very much. Some islanders did not even know that there were other islands nearby. Travel among the islands was hard because islands were thousands of miles apart. It took a long time to travel between islands in small boats. Many times, there was little communication between the people of the same island. Thick forests and mountains made it hard for people on an island to communicate with one another. The people living on the thousands of islands in the archipelago spoke more than 200 different languages.

It has been hard for the islands of Indonesia to be a united nation, even in modern times. Airplane and ship travel is now possible. But this kind of transportation is

◀ Indonesia exports many crops, such as tea.

113

too expensive for most Indonesians. It is hard for people on different islands to visit each other.

The people of Indonesia have formed one united nation. Today, Indonesians still speak many different languages. But many people also speak the nation's official language, called Bahasa Indonesia. Children now learn to speak this language in schools. On all the islands, people now use one kind of currency, or money. One president leads the people of all the nation's islands. The religion of Islam joins most Indonesians together.

Today Indonesia earns most of its money by exporting different products. The nation earns more money from oil than from any other export. Indonesia is a member of OPEC. The nation also sells tin, lumber, and cash crops to other nations. Rubber is the most important cash crop. Cocoa, coffee, and tea are other important exports.

Most people in Indonesia are subsistence farmers. Slash-and-burn farming and wet rice farming are used in different regions. The nation's average income is about $600 a year. Most people have a low standard of living.

Indonesians on thousands of islands have worked hard to form one nation. Today millions of people share the same language, religion, money, and government.

▶ Indonesia makes a lot of money from exporting oil.

Using What You Learned

▼ **Read and Remember —— Write the Answer**

Write sentences to answer the questions.

1. What is an archipelago? _____

   _____

2. How does volcanic ash help Java? _____

   _____

3. When did Indonesia become a nation? _____

4. What are two things that make it hard for the Indonesian islands to be

   a nation? _____

   _____

5. What are three things that help the Indonesian islands form one nation?

   _____

6. What is Indonesia's most important export? _____

▼ **Think and Apply —— Compare and Contrast**

Read each sentence below. Does it tell how Thailand and Indonesia are alike?
Does it tell how they are different? Write an **A** before the statement if it
tells how these two nations are alike. Write a **D** before the statement if it
tells how the nations are different.

_____ 1. There are thousands of islands.

_____ 2. It has a tropical climate.

_____ 3. There are monsoon rains.

_____ 4. Oil is the most important export.

_____ 5. Rice is the most important export.

_____ 6. It has always been a free nation.

_____ 7. Most people are farmers.

_____ 8. It is a developing nation.

▼ Skill Builder —— Reviewing Tables

Use the facts from the table to match each sentence with the correct answer.

Facts About India, Indonesia, and Thailand					
Nation	Population of Nation	Capital	Population of Capital	Longest River	Length of Longest River
India	844 million	New Delhi	600,000	Ganges	1,557 miles
Indonesia	188 million	Jakarta	9 million	Kapuas	450 miles
Thailand	56 million	Bangkok	6 million	Chao Phraya	227 miles

1. New Delhi has a population of _____.

2. The shortest river is the _____.

3. The capital with the largest population is _____.

4. The length of the Ganges River is _____.

5. The population of Thailand is _____.

6. The nation with the smallest population is _____.

7. The nation with the largest population is _____.

a. 56 million

b. 1,557 miles

c. 600,000

d. Thailand

e. India

f. Chao Phraya

g. Jakarta

Chapter Fifteen

Problems Facing South and Southeast Asia

NEW WORDS

human labor
overpopulation
deforestation

South and Southeast Asia is the most populated region in the world. Many people in this region do not get enough to eat. The large population and hunger are two serious problems in this region. How are nations solving these problems? What are two other problems facing this region? The answers are in this chapter.

The first problem is hunger. It is hard for the nations of South and Southeast Asia to grow enough food. In many places, farmers do not use modern methods. They use **human labor** and farm animals because they do not have enough money to buy modern farm machines. Another reason is that farmers depend on rain from the

POPULATION OF SOUTH AND SOUTHEAST ASIA

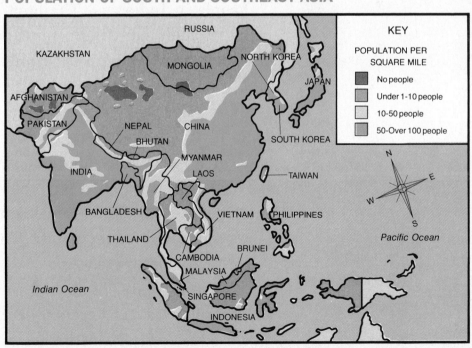

▶ The monsoon rains can cause serious flooding in South and Southeast Asia.

monsoon winds to help them grow food. Sometimes there is too much rain, and rivers flood. But the monsoons do not always bring heavy rains. Sometimes there are droughts. In those years, the farmers do not grow enough food to feed the nation. Another reason these nations cannot grow enough food for their people is that the tropical forests and the high mountains are not good for farming.

People in India and Thailand have worked to end hunger. They have built dams on rivers to hold water for irrigation. This gives farmers a supply of water all the time. But making dams can cause problems, too. Remember that rivers carry a natural fertilizer called silt. Without silt coming down the rivers, the soil gets less and less fertile. Many subsistence farmers do not have enough money to buy chemical fertilizers. With a dammed-up river, they have water for their crops, but their soil is no longer fertile. Then they are not able to grow as many crops.

For many years, India had to import wheat. Today in northern India, farmers are using better wheat seeds, more fertilizers, and better tools. India now grows enough wheat for its people. Sometimes, there is extra wheat that can be exported. But many farmers are still too poor to buy better seeds and fertilizers.

Overpopulation is the second problem in South and Southeast Asia. The populations of most nations are growing very fast. There is not enough farmland in the region to farm crops for the growing population. In many nations, the population will double in about 30 years. This means there will be twice as many people in 30 years. India will have more than one billion people!

So governments are trying to teach people to have smaller families. Governments use radio and television to tell people how to have smaller families. In areas without modern communication, the governments send teachers to tell people to plan the size of their families. But in many Asian cultures, people are proud to have large families. They want to have children to help with wet rice farming. Many Asian people cannot read and write and do not understand how to have smaller families. Overpopulation is a hard problem to solve. But until population growth is slowed down, people in the region will continue to be hungry.

Deforestation is the third problem in South and Southeast Asia. Deforestation means the forests of a

◄ The population of Southeast Asia is growing very fast.

region are being destroyed. Many thick tropical forests have been chopped down. Trees are chopped down by farmers who do slash and burn farming. Other trees are chopped down because people use wood for fuel. Many trees are chopped down and used for lumber that can be exported.

What happens when forests are destroyed? Many kinds of wildlife live in these forests. The wild animals die when their forest homes are destroyed. When forests are destroyed, fertile soil is washed away by heavy rains. Without fertile soil, it is harder for farmers to grow enough food. Some nations are trying to stop the deforestation. They are planting new trees to replace the trees that are cut down.

Wars and political unrest are the fourth problem in this region. In some nations, such as India and Pakistan, religious groups are fighting one another. Most people in India are Hindus. And most Pakistanis are Muslims. Each nation wants to control land that belongs to the other nation.

In other nations, such as Vietnam, there have been wars between Communists and non-Communists. In

▶ Many forests in South and Southeast Asia have been destroyed.

◀ Religious groups in India and Pakistan are fighting each other.

Vietnam, the fighting lasted almost 20 years. Many farms, factories, villages, and jungles were destroyed. Many people were killed or forced to leave their villages. In 1975, the Communists won and Vietnam became a communist nation. Vietnam has had a hard time rebuilding the nation since the war.

South and Southeast Asia is a developing region with more than one and a half billion people. This region also has fertile soil, long rivers, and many natural resources. It has the resources it needs to have a much higher standard of living. Many nations are spending money to build more schools and hospitals. Foreign businesses are investing money to build modern factories. Many nations are now growing much more food than ever before. Now the people of this region must find new ways to work for peace. With peace, people can work together for a better life in this crowded part of the world.

Using What You Learned

▼ **Read and Remember —— Find the Answer**

Put a check (✔) next to the sentences below that tell about the problems of Southeast Asia. You should check five sentences.

_____ 1. There is not enough food.

_____ 2. Not enough people work at farming.

_____ 3. Many forests are destroyed.

_____ 4. Many people are hungry.

_____ 5. People eat too much rice.

_____ 6. There is overpopulation.

_____ 7. There have been years of war and fighting.

_____ 8. There are many large deserts.

▼ **Think and Apply —— Analogies**

Use a word in dark print to finish each sentence.

Bangkok **Vietnam** **Hinduism**
Indonesia **overpopulation** **deforestation**

1. New Delhi is to India as _____ is to Thailand.

2. Building dams is to not enough rain as planting trees is to _____.

3. Modern machines are to hunger as smaller families are to _____.

4. Fighting between Communists and non-Communists is to _____ as fighting between Hindus and Muslims is to India and Pakistan.

5. Buddhism is to Thailand as _____ is to India.

6. Rice is to Thailand as oil is to _____.

122

▼ Skill Builder —— Reading a Population Map

A population map shows where people live in a region. It also shows the population density of a region. The map can show which areas are densely populated because they have many people. They show which areas have a lower population density because they have fewer people. The map key on a population map helps you learn the population of a region.

Look at the population map of South and Southeast Asia on page 117. Write **T** next to each sentence that is true. Write **F** next to each sentence that is false. There are three false sentences. On the lines below, rewrite the false sentences to make them true.

_____ 1. There are 50 to more than 100 people in a square mile in southern India.

_____ 2. Some parts of western India have under ten people in a square mile.

_____ 3. Mongolia is densely populated.

_____ 4. The eastern island of Indonesia has a low population density.

_____ 5. Parts of China have no people.

_____ 6. Every part of Thailand has under 50 people in a square mile.

_____ 7. Little of Japan is densely populated.

_____

_____

_____

Mt. Everest

The two men struggled to put one foot after the other. The slope was very steep. Ice and snow lay all around. A cold wind blew.

Suddenly the men reached the top. Edmund Hillary and Tenzing Norgay had climbed the world's tallest mountain. They had reached the top of Mt. Everest. They were the first people to climb to the top of Mt. Everest.

Only about 100 others have made the same climb. But thousands of people visit Mt. Everest each year.

THE HIMALAYA

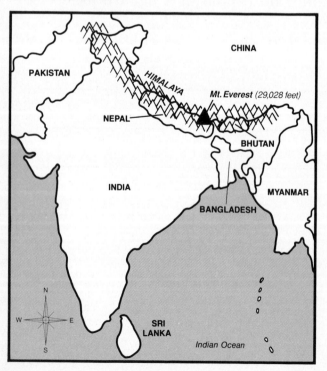

Mt. Everest is in trouble. The people who visit it are hurting the land.

Location/Place

Mt. Everest is on the border between the nations of China and Nepal. It is over five miles high—the tallest mountain in the world. Other tall mountains are all around. The thin air makes it hard to breathe.

These mountains are one of the most beautiful places in the world. The land is very rough. Hills are steep. Valleys are narrow and deep. Nothing grows near the top, but there are trees, grass, and animals lower down.

Human/Environment Interaction

Just a few years ago, only a few people visited Nepal. Today, there are thousands of visitors each year.

These visitors need places to stay and food to eat. The people of Nepal are cutting down their forests to build houses and hotels and to make fires to keep the visitors warm. The visitors also leave behind trash.

A national park has been set up around Mt. Everest. It is against the law to cut trees in the park. But people cut the trees anyway. Soil once held by tree roots is washing away.

Movement

The people of Nepal want people to visit their country and spend money. Many people in Nepal earn money by helping the visitors. They show them where to go. There are no roads in the mountains, only walking trails. In ten years, a million people a year might visit Nepal.

People are trying to keep Mt. Everest from being spoiled. The problem is that people keep visiting it. Some visitors carry their trash away with them. Most throw trash by the trails. How can the beauty of Nepal and Mt. Everest be saved?

▲ These mountain climbers look at Mt. Everest.

Write About It

Suppose that you are planning a trip to Mt. Everest. You must carry your food with you. Plan what you would take to eat. Explain how you could cut down on the amount of trash you would have to get rid of.

_____

_____

_____

_____

_____

_____

East Asia
and the Pacific

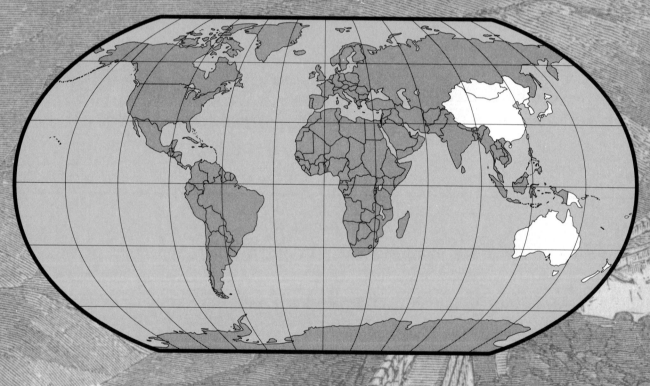

Dear Uncle Phillippe,

There are so many people everywhere. I've never seen such big crowds! You can't believe how many different ways people here eat rice! We leave Asia tomorrow to fly to Australia. I'm looking foward to it.

Love, Cecile

POST CARD
AIR MAIL

100 NIPPON

Phillippe Belmont
141 Cascade Drive
Seattle, Washington
U.S.A. 98107

Chapter Sixteen

Looking at East Asia and the Pacific

NEW WORDS

mainland
coral reefs
natural disasters
earthquakes
typhoons

American stores are filled with products from East Asia and the Pacific. Stores sell bicycles from Taiwan, watches from Hong Kong, and computers from Japan. You can buy baskets and cotton dresses made in China. Other stores sell wool sweaters from Australia. Each of these goods gives you a small picture of the nation where it was made. Many areas in East Asia and the Pacific have modern urban industries. Other areas have cottage industries and small farms. There are many ways people live and work in these nations. As you read this unit, look for ways that nations in this region are different from one another.

▶ Workers in East Asia make goods to export all over the world.

Find East Asia and the Pacific on the map below. Notice that the Equator divides the region into two parts. North of the Equator is East Asia. This is the eastern part of the **mainland**, or continent, of Asia. North Korea, South Korea, and China are all on the mainland. Japan and Taiwan are two island nations near the mainland, in the Pacific Ocean. Find each of these nations on the map below.

South of the Equator is a group of about 25,000 islands called Oceania. Some islands in Oceania are just north of the Equator. There are so many tiny islands in this region that no one has ever counted them. Find Oceania on the map below. Notice that New Guinea and the two islands of New Zealand are the three largest islands in Oceania.

EAST ASIA AND THE PACIFIC

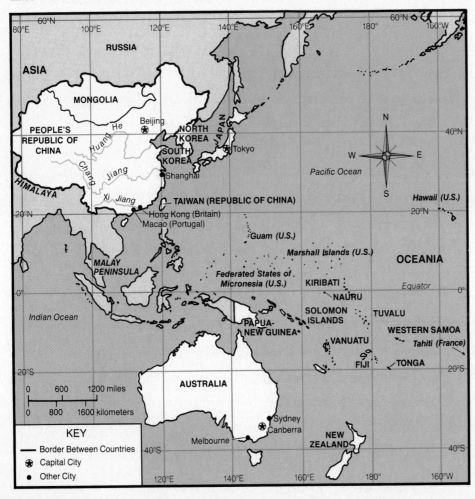

▲ This island is on a coral reef.

The continent of Australia is also south of the Equator. Australia is between the Indian and Pacific oceans. In all parts of the world, places south of the Equator have seasons that are opposite the seasons in the north. When it is winter in the Southern Hemisphere, it is summer in the Northern Hemisphere.

There are two kinds of islands in the Pacific. There are low islands and high islands. These two kinds of islands were formed in different ways. Low islands were built up slowly over time. High islands were formed in a shorter time by volcanoes.

Low islands are made of **coral reefs**. A coral reef is made from the skeletons of tiny sea animals. These small animals build their homes on top of one another and form reefs. Some reefs look like large rocks that are just below the water. Some low islands are only a few feet above the level of the sea. There is not much soil on these islands, so it is hard to grow food crops.

High islands were made by volcanoes. These islands have a mountain in the middle of the island. Many of these volcanoes do not erupt anymore. The islands of New Zealand are high islands.

The region also has other landforms. The high Himalaya are in southwestern China. High mountains cover many other parts of China. Mountains cover most of Japan, Korea, and Taiwan. East Asia also has lowlands near the coasts and rivers. Most East Asians live in these crowded lowlands and in fertile river valleys. Some of the river valleys in China have been used for farming for thousands of years. Much of Australia is covered with flat plains and plateaus. But few people live on the large plains in Australia.

There are different climates in different parts of East Asia and the Pacific. Winters in some parts of East Asia are cold and dry because of monsoon winds that come from the icy arctic north. Summers in most of East Asia are hot and rainy because the monsoons bring rain from the ocean. Coastal areas receive the most rain. Inland areas are drier. Parts of western China have a desert climate because they receive so little rain.

Most of the Pacific islands are near the Equator. So these islands have warm, tropical weather all year. But mountains on some of these islands are so tall that they have snow on top all year long. Some Pacific islands get only a few inches of rain a year. Most of Australia is very dry. Other islands like New Zealand get lots of rain.

◀ This Pacific island has a warm, tropical climate.

Natural disasters are part of life in many areas of East Asia and the Pacific. Natural disasters are terrible accidents caused by nature. Japan, Taiwan, and many Pacific islands have volcanoes that erupt from time to time. These areas also have **earthquakes**. During an earthquake, the ground shakes and the land may crack. When this happens, earthquakes can destroy buildings and bridges. People are sometimes killed by buildings and trees that are knocked down. Some islands are hit by wet tropical storms called **typhoons**. High winds, rough seas, and heavy rains come with typhoons. Typhoons can destroy many buildings.

There are developed and developing nations in East Asia and the Pacific. China and most of the Pacific islands are developing nations. In these nations, most people are subsistence farmers. Even though China has heavy industries and mines, it makes few consumer goods. Japan, Taiwan, Australia, and New Zealand are important developed nations. Many people live in cities and have a high standard of living.

Some nations in this region have free market economies where companies decide what to produce. Communist nations like China and North Korea have command

▶ This damage was caused by a big earthquake in China.

132

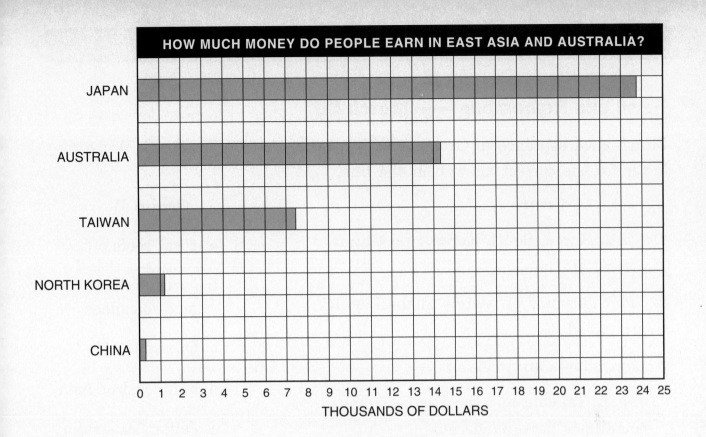

HOW MUCH MONEY DO PEOPLE EARN IN EAST ASIA AND AUSTRALIA?

JAPAN

AUSTRALIA

TAIWAN

NORTH KOREA

CHINA

0 1 2 3 4 5 6 7 8 9 10 11 12 13 14 15 16 17 18 19 20 21 22 23 24 25

THOUSANDS OF DOLLARS

economies. In these nations, the government decides what factories should make and what farmers should grow. Some nations are between these two kinds of economies. The governments of some nations, such as Japan, decide on the number of some products that can be produced and imported. The Japanese government decides how many trees can be cut down for lumber and how many foreign cars can be imported.

People in the region belong to different cultural, religious, and ethnic groups. They speak dozens of different languages that use different ways of writing words. Buddhism is an important religion in East Asia. Most people in Australia and New Zealand are Christians.

You will be reading about China, Japan, and Australia in this unit. As you read, try to find out why eastern China is more crowded than western China. Find out how Japan became an industrial leader. Learn why Australia has more sheep than people.

Using What You Learned

▼ Read and Remember —— Match Up

Finish each sentence in Group A with an answer from Group B. Write the letter for the correct answer on the line.

Group A

1. North Korea, South Korea, and China are all on the ____.

2. The thousands of islands in the Pacific are called ____.

3. Low islands are made of ____.

4. Japan, Taiwan, and the Pacific islands sometimes have dangerous ____.

5. Most of the Pacific islands have a ____.

6. Three nations with a high standard of living are ____.

Group B

a. coral reefs

b. earthquakes and volcanoes

c. Oceania

d. mainland of Asia

e. Japan, Australia, and New Zealand

f. warm climate

▼ Skill Builder —— Reviewing Bar Graphs

The bar graph on page 133 shows the amount of money people earn in five nations of East Asia and the Pacific. Look at all the bars. Then write the answer to each question.

1. In which nation do people earn the least money?_____

2. In which nation do people earn the most money?_____

3. In which two nations do people earn less than $2,000 a year?

_____

4. Which nation do you think has the lowest standard of living? _____

5. Which two nations do you think have the highest standard of living?

_____

▼ Think and Apply —— Exclusions

One word in each group does not belong. Find that word, and cross it out.
Then write a sentence that tells how the other words are alike.

1. Japan   _____

    China   _____

    Taiwan   _____

    Oceania   _____

2. Australia   _____

    New Zealand   _____

    Korea   _____

    25,000 Pacific islands _____

3. North Korea   _____

    South Korea   _____

    China   _____

    Australia   _____

4. rainfall   _____

    typhoons   _____

    volcanoes   _____

    earthquakes   _____

Chapter Seventeen

China: A Nation with a Large Population

NEW WORDS

production
contracts

protests

China is a developing nation with the world's largest population. Two thirds of China's people are farmers. China is only a little larger than the United States, but it has four times as many people. How is China able to feed so many people?

Find China on the map on page 137. Find the Himalaya Mountains in the southwest. Notice the Huang He, Chang, and Xi rivers in eastern China. Most people live in the lowlands around these three important rivers. The British colony of Hong Kong is near the mouth of

▼ There are many farms in the fertile lowlands of China.

136

the Xi River. Hong Kong will be ruled by China in 1997. The island nation of Taiwan is to the east of China. This island was ruled by China until 1949.

China's history began 5000 years ago. Just like today, people of long ago farmed the fertile valleys of the Huang He, Chang, and Xi rivers.

China today is a communist nation. It became a communist nation in 1949 after a long civil war. During the civil war, Communists and non-Communists fought against each other. Millions of Chinese wanted the Communists to win because so many people were poor and hungry. In 1949, the Communists won the civil war. The non-Communists escaped to the island of Taiwan. Since 1949, non-Communist Chinese have ruled Taiwan.

China has four large regions. About one fourth of China's people live in the region of Southern China. Southern China is an important agricultural area. The Chang and Xi rivers flow through Southern China. The soil around these rivers is very fertile. Millions of

CHINA

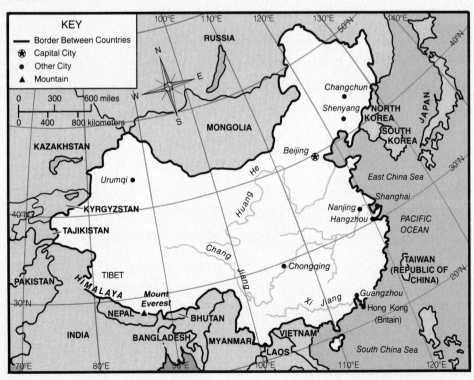

CLIMATE MAP OF CHINA

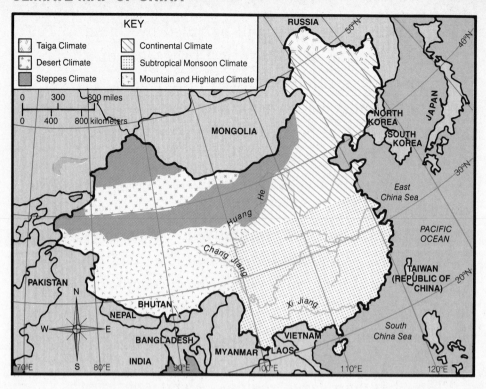

people live on the lowlands near these rivers. The climate is warm and humid. Summer monsoons bring plenty of rain. A lot of rice is grown in this area. Farmers also grow tea, cotton, fruits, and vegetables. Southern China also has large industrial cities. China's largest city, Shanghai, is a port in Southern China. Shanghai has 12 million people. It is one of the most crowded cities in the world.

Northern China is another crowded region. The Huang He River flows through Northern China. This river often has dangerous floods. For thousands of years, the Chinese have worked hard to control the floods and to protect their homes and farms. Northern China has a continental climate. Winters are long and cold. Summers are short and hot. It is too cool for rice farming. Wheat is the most important crop in Northern China.

Beijing is the most important industrial city in Northern China. It is China's capital. Beijing is near large iron and coal mines. Factories in Beijing use iron and coal to make steel. Other factories use steel to make machines, weapons, and airplanes.

The Northeast region is an important industrial area. Oil, coal, and iron are this region's important minerals. The standard of living is higher in the Northeast than in other parts of China. But few people live in the Northeast.

Western China has one third of China's land. But it has the smallest population. There are very high mountains in the north, west, and south. A very high plateau covers other parts of the region. This region gets so little rain that there are two large deserts.

More than one billion people live in China today. It is hard to grow food and care for this huge population. So the government is trying to keep the population from growing too fast. The government asks couples not to marry before they are in their 20s and to have only one or two children.

The communist government tries to make sure farmers grow more food each year. So the government makes **production contracts** with each family. In these contracts, farmers agree to grow some crops for the government. Families try hard to grow more than what they must give the government. If a family grows more

▼ Many people in Beijing, the capital of China, use bicycles.

▲ Thousands of students protested against the Chinese government in 1989.

food, they may keep it or sell it. Most Chinese people now have enough food to live. This system has helped China's farming villages to have a higher standard of living.

In cities, people live in more modern homes and apartments than people in rural areas. But they have less living space. People in cities have a higher standard of living than rural Chinese people have.

China's one billion people live in a nation that allows very little freedom. People are not allowed to speak, write, or work against the communist government. Since the 1980s, many people have demanded more freedom. In 1989, thousands of Beijing students started **protests** against the government. People in other cities also protested that they wanted more freedom. The government sent the army to attack the protesting students. Many Beijing students were killed. The protests ended. The Chinese did not win freedom from their communist leaders.

China would like to become a modern nation with a higher standard of living. China has a lot more work to do to become a developed nation. No one knows how China will change during the next few years. Newspapers will continue to tell us about important changes in this nation of one billion people.

Using What You Learned

Choose a word in dark print to finish each sentence. Write the word on the correct blank.

Western China   **agricultural   farmers   Beijing**
command economy   industrial   Shanghai   billion

1. Two thirds of the people in China work as _____.

2. China has more than one _____ people.

3. China has a _____ in which the government controls most factories and businesses.

4. The largest city in China is _____.

5. Mountains, deserts, and high plateaus cover _____.

6. The capital of China is the city of _____.

7. The Northeast region is an important _____ area.

8. Southern China is an important _____ area.

▼ **Think and Apply —— Fact or Opinion**

Read each sentence below. Write an **F** next to each sentence that tells a fact. Write an **O** next to each sentence that tells an opinion. You should find three sentences that are opinions.

_____ 1. For thousands of years, the Chinese have farmed the land around the Chang, Huang He, and Xi rivers.

_____ 2. Chinese Communists won the civil war in 1949.

_____ 3. China has better leaders than Taiwan has.

_____ 4. One fourth of China's people live in Southern China.

_____ 5. Chinese farmers grow rice in the south and wheat in the North.

_____ 6. Chinese farmers should grow more wheat.

_____ 7. Western China has the most beautiful land in China.

_____ 8. Chinese students protested against the government in 1989.

▼ Skill Builder —— Reviewing Climate Maps

The map on page 138 shows six climates that are found in China.

taiga climate: long, cold, snowy winters and very short, mild summers

continental climate: cold, dry winters and hot, humid summers

subtropical monsoon climate: cool, dry winters and hot, rainy summers

desert climate: dry weather all year

steppes climate: dry weather with about 15 inches of rain during the year

mountain and highland climate: rainy or snowy winters and dry summers

Look at the climate map on page 138. Then finish each sentence with a word in dark print.

northeast   **mountain and highland**
west   **southeast**   **taiga**

1. China has a _____ climate in the Northeast near Russia.

2. Most of the _____ has a continental climate.

3. The _____ has a subtropical monsoon climate.

4. China has a desert climate in the _____.

5. In the southwest, China has a _____ climate.

Chapter Eighteen

Japan: An Industrial Leader

NEW WORDS

nuclear energy
electronic
balance of trade
kimono

The United States, Japan, and other nations fought each other in World War II. The United States wanted to stop Japan from fighting any longer. In August, 1945, the United States dropped an atomic bomb on a Japanese city. The bomb destroyed much of the city and

JAPAN

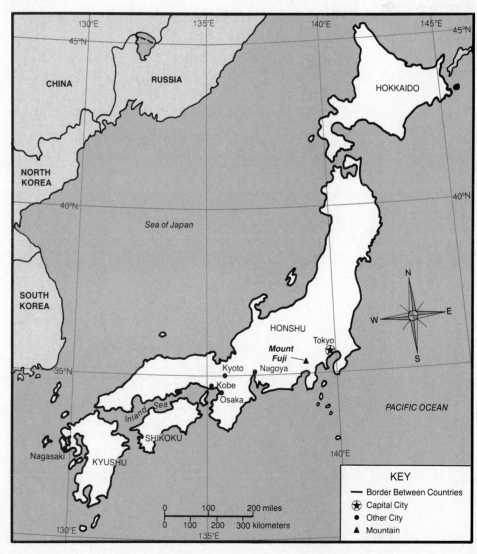

killed about 92,000 people. Three days later, an even larger atomic bomb destroyed the industries and port of another city. Soon Japan said it would no longer fight against the United States and other nations.

World War II was over, and much of Japan lay in ruins. But in a few years, the Japanese had rebuilt their nation's industries. The United States had helped Japan to rebuild. The Japanese put modern technology in their new factories. So the new Japanese industries were even better than the ones that had been destroyed. Today, Japan is one of the world's industrial leaders. Industries from nations all over the world study Japan's factories to learn how the Japanese make good products. As you read this chapter, think about how Japan could have changed so much in less than 50 years.

Find Japan on the map on page 143. Notice that Japan is an archipelago nation between the Pacific Ocean and the Sea of Japan. Find the nation's four main islands. Japan has thousands of small islands, too.

Japan has few natural resources, so it depends on the sea. The Japanese eat fish and seaweed. Japan trades with other nations. There are many harbors along the

▼ This Japanese volcano is called Mt. Fuji.

▲ Most Japanese live in cities on the island of Honshu.

coast that Japan can use for shipping and trade.

Mountains and coastal plains are the two main landforms in Japan. Mountains and hills with thick forests cover most of Japan. Japan has about 60 volcanoes that sometimes erupt. The highest and most famous mountain is a volcano called Mt. Fuji. Japan has many short, fast rivers. The rivers are good for making hydroelectric power and for irrigating farmland.

Since most of Japan is covered with rough mountains and forests, most people live on the east coast of the island of Honshu. Honshu's coastal plains have most of Japan's farms, factories, and cities. Tokyo, Japan's capital and largest city, is in these lowlands. The other three main islands have only small areas that can be used for farming and industries. So these other islands have small populations.

Japan's climate is different from south to north. Islands in the south have hot summers and mild winters. These southern islands have the best climate for farming. The northern islands have cool summers and cold winters with some snow. The island of Honshu has warm, humid summers and cold winters.

Japan has few natural resources for its factories.

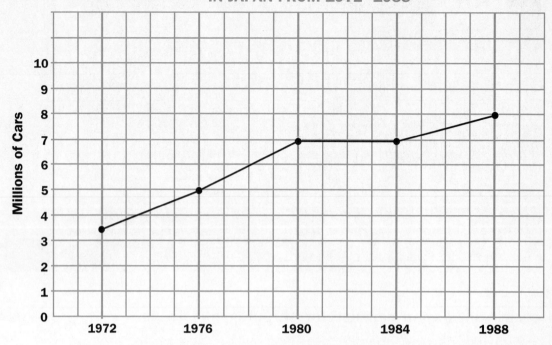

Japan imports the minerals and raw materials it needs from many nations. It imports coal and iron to make steel. It imports huge amounts of oil from the Middle East to make electricity and gasoline.

Japan does not like to depend on other nations for all of its energy. Japan now makes some of its electricity from **nuclear energy**. It also uses water to make hydroelectric power.

The most important natural resource in Japan is its hard-working people. The Japanese culture teaches people to work hard and to do their best. Japan's workers are trained to make cars, cameras, computers, and many electronic products. Radios and televisions are electronic products.

Each year, Japanese factories add new kinds of technology. And workers develop new products that work better or cost less to make. Developed nations must work hard to keep up with Japanese industries.

Today Japan has a very good **balance of trade**. This means that Japan earns more from its exports than it spends on its imports. Japan must import food, oil, and raw materials. This nation does not import many factory products. It exports electronic products, cars, and many other goods.

Japanese farmers are also able to produce many crops with few resources. Even though there is very little farmland, Japan produces about two thirds of the food its people need.

Japan has many modern, industrial cities. Tokyo is the nation's capital. It is the center of banking and industry for Japan. It is also a very busy port.

Modern ways of life and traditional culture can be seen together in Japan. Many people wear western style clothes. But many Japanese also wear traditional clothes, such as a long robe called a **kimono**.

Japan is a crowded island nation with about 123 million people. After World War II, these hard-working people helped make their nation strong again. In a short time, Japan has become one of the world's leaders in industry and technology.

▼ Tokyo is one of the largest cities in the world.

Using What You Learned

▼ **Think and Apply —— Cause and Effect**

Match each cause on the left with an effect on the right. Write the letter of the effect on the correct blank.

Cause

1. Japan was destroyed during World War II, so _____.

2. Japan has few natural resources, so _____.

3. Japan has a long coast with many ports, so _____.

4. Japanese farmers are able to grow a lot of crops, so _____.

5. Japan exports more than it imports, so _____.

6. The Japanese love their old traditions, so _____.

Effect

a. it must import natural resources for its factories.

b. Japan has a good balance of trade.

c. it is easy to import raw materials and export factory goods.

d. they wear traditional clothes as well as modern ones.

e. there is food for about two thirds of Japan's people.

f. the Japanese had to work hard to rebuild their nation.

▼ **Read and Remember —— Write the Answer**

Write an answer to each question.

1. Why is Japan an archipelago?

_____

2. Which island has the most people?

_____

3. What are Japan's two main landforms?

_____

4. What products does Japan import?

_____

5. What does Japan export?

_____

6. Why is Japan an important nation?

_____

▼ Skill Builder —— Reviewing Line Graphs

The line graph on page 146 shows the number of cars that were manufactured in Japan between 1972 and 1988.

Finish each sentence in Group A with an answer from Group B.

Group A	Group B
1. The smallest number of cars was made in _____.	a. 5 million
2. The largest number of cars was made in _____.	b. 7 million
3. Between 1980 and 1984, the number of cars made each year was about _____.	c. 1972 d. grew larger
4. In 1976, Japan made _____ cars.	e. 1988
5. From 1972 to 1988, the number of cars that were manufactured _____.	f. stayed the same
6. From 1980 to 1984, the number of cars that were manufactured _____.	

Chapter Nineteen

Australia: A Dry Continent

NEW WORDS

reservations

uranium

nuclear
weapons

livestock

outback

artesian wells

compete

▼ The capital city
of Canberra is
where Australia's
government meets.

Which nation covers a whole continent? Which nation has almost ten times more sheep than people? The answer to these questions is the continent of Australia. In this chapter, you will learn how people live on the world's driest continent.

Find Australia on the map on page 151. Notice that Australia is surrounded by the Pacific Ocean and the Indian Ocean. Australia has six states and two territories. The Australia Capital Territory is around the capital, Canberra. Tasmania, an island south of Australia, is one state.

Most of Australia is low and flat. The continent has three landform regions. The Western Plateau covers the

western part of Australia. It is the largest region. Two deserts cover most of the plateau. The outer parts of the plateau have short grass and bushes. Cattle and sheep graze there.

The Central Lowlands are just east of the Western Plateau. Some areas of this dry, flat land have enough grass to feed cattle and sheep. Also, miners dig for minerals in two towns in this dry region. But this region does not have big cities because it gets very little rain.

The Eastern Highlands are the third region. This region goes from the Great Dividing Range to the Pacific Ocean. The Great Dividing Range is a group of mountains that goes from the north to the south. The Eastern Highlands has high plateaus, hills, and low mountains. Forests cover parts of the Eastern Highlands. East of the Great Dividing Range, near the Pacific Ocean, are coastal plains that receive much rain.

AUSTRALIA

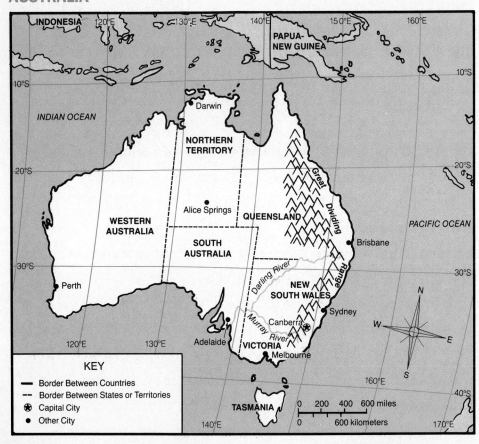

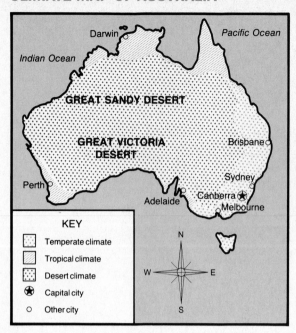

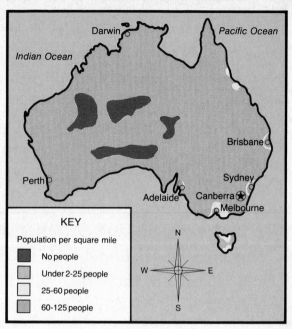

Farmers produce many of the nation's crops here. Wheat is the nation's most important crop.

Most Australians live in the southeastern coastal plains. There, the climate is milder than it is in the tropical north. The nation's two largest cities, Sydney and Melbourne, are in this region. Each of these port cities has a population of over 3 million. Canberra, Australia's capital, is also in this region.

The first people to live in Australia were Aborigines. Only a few Aborigines, or native Australians, are alive today. Many live in poor urban neighborhoods or on government **reservations** in rural areas. A few Aborigines live in their traditional ways. Most Australians have a high standard of living. And most Australians have British ancestors who came to the continent starting in the 1700s.

Australia does not have much water, but it is rich in other resources. The nation mines coal, copper, iron, and lead and sells these resources to Japan and other nations. Today, Australians mine copper, diamonds, and coal. Australians also have iron, oil, and natural gas.

Australia wants to develop mining. But many

Australians believe that mining and transporting one of their main resources, **uranium**, is unsafe. Uranium is used to make nuclear energy and **nuclear weapons**. Other Australians think that the beauty of rural areas would be ruined by mining. And other people do not think it is fair to mine minerals that are found on the Aborigines' reservations. This will be an important decision for Australians in the years to come.

Australia also earns a lot of money from raising **livestock**, such as sheep and cattle. This nation exports a lot of meat from these animals. Also, Australia exports more wool than any other nation.

Ranchers raise livestock in the dry interior, or **outback**, of Australia. Very few people live in the outback because it is so hot and dry. Livestock drink the water from **artesian wells** in the outback. People dig artesian wells to get to water that is stored under the ground. The underground water comes up without being pumped.

Ranchers have a high standard of living, but they live far from other people. There are few roads that connect the ranches to the nation's cities. Many ranchers use small airplanes to travel from one place to another.

▼ This is a big sheep farm in Australia.

▶ This airport is in the outback of Australia.

Children on ranches live very far from most schools. So they learn at home by listening to special radio programs called Schools of the Air.

Although much of Australia's land is used for raising livestock, most people in the nation work in cities. Most Australians have service jobs at stores, hospitals, schools, and banks. Many Australians work in factories that make cloth, chemicals, cars, and consumer goods.

Few of Australia's factory goods are exported. There are several reasons why. First, Australia is far from its main trading partners, Japan and the United States. Australia's goods become more expensive because it is expensive to ship them so far away. Second, Australia's trading partners are developed nations. These nations need Australia's raw materials for their own factories. Japan and the United States do not want Australians to send them goods that would **compete** with products from their own factories.

Australia is a large continent with lots of dry, empty land. Perhaps one day, Australians will find a way to bring water into their dry interior. Until that happens, Australia will be a large nation with a small population.

Using What You Learned

▼ **Read and Remember —— Writing Workshop**

Write a paragraph that tells where people live in Australia and why they live there. Give at least 3 examples that show how the people earn money.

_____

_____

_____

_____

_____

_____

_____

_____

▼ **Think and Apply —— Finding the Main Idea**

Read each group of sentences below. One of the sentences is a main idea. Two of the sentences support the main idea. Write an **M** next to the sentence that is the main idea in each group.

1. _____ a. The southeast gets plenty of rain.

   _____ b. There are cities in the southeast.

   _____ c. Most Australians live in the southeast.

2. _____ a. The Great Dividing Range is in the east.

   _____ b. Australia has three landform regions.

   _____ c. The Central Lowlands and the Western Plateau cover most of Australia.

3. _____ a. Australia has coal and iron.

_____ b. The nation has uranium, copper, and diamonds.

_____ c. Australia has many minerals.

4. _____ a. Sheep are very important in Australia.

_____ b. Australia exports meat from sheep.

_____ c. Australia exports more wool than any other nation.

5. _____ a. The outback is very hot and dry.

_____ b. Few people choose to live in the outback.

_____ c. There are few natural resources in the outback.

▼ Skill Builder —— Comparing Maps

We can learn more about Australia by comparing two kinds of maps. Look at the population and climate maps of Australia on page 152. Look at the southeast of Australia on both maps. The climate map shows a **temperate climate** in the southeast. The population map shows a dense population in the southeast. By comparing the two maps, we learn that more people live in the southeast where there is a temperate climate than in any other part of the nation.

Write **T** next to each sentence that is true. Write **F** next to each sentence that is false.

_____ 1. Canberra and Brisbane have a tropical climate.

_____ 2. Many people live on the west coast.

_____ 3. Darwin has a tropical climate.

_____ 4. More people live in a temperate climate than in a desert climate.

_____ 5. Many people live in the northern tropical climate.

_____ 6. Most of Australia has a desert climate.

Chapter Twenty

The Future of East Asia and the Pacific

NEW WORDS

tremors
dikes
environment
Confucians

The nations of East Asia and the Pacific have one fourth of the world's people. Big differences in standards of living can be seen in this region. In some nations, like Japan and Australia, people enjoy a high standard of living. Other countries, like China, are poor, developing nations that need more industries and new technology. The nations of this region share four problems today. In this chapter, you will learn how nations are trying to solve these problems.

One problem that all nations share is natural disasters. In China, dangerous floods kill people and ruin crops.

► The Huang He River in China often floods.

Even though the rivers can be dangerous, people live near them so they can farm on all of the fertile farmland. The Huang He floods about once in every five years. The floods of the Huang He River have killed many people.

Japan has a different kind of natural disaster because of its location. Japan is on the edge of a huge piece of land that is under water. This land moves from time to time, and this moving causes earthquakes and volcanoes along the land's edge. Japan has about 1500 small earthquakes, or **tremors**, each year. When earthquakes happen under water, they can make dangerous waves that destroy land along the coast.

The Chinese and Japanese have tried to stop the damage caused by these disasters. Today, most floods are stopped by dams and **dikes**. Dikes are short walls of dirt and rocks. The Japanese have also built cities so that earthquakes cause less damage. Buildings are made so that they do not break apart during an earthquake.

Australia's natural disasters come from its dry climate. Australia has only two rivers that can be used for irrigation. So droughts cause crops to dry up and die. Huge fires in Australia's grasslands also cause problems for ranchers and wild animals. Many areas do not have

▶ This dike was built to stop a flooding river.

enough water to put out large fires. Sometimes fires destroy many miles of grassland. When the grass and bushes are destroyed, it is easy for wind to erode the soil. Then it is hard for animals to find food.

A second problem in East Asia and the Pacific is the struggle between communist and non-communist governments. China and North Korea are the two communist nations of this region. Korea was divided into two nations in 1948. North Korea became a communist nation, and South Korea became a non-communist nation. In 1950, the Communists of North Korea attacked South Korea. Soldiers from many nations helped South Korea stay a separate nation from North Korea. Will China and North Korea someday give up communism?

Another big change will come to China in 1997. In that year, Hong Kong will become a part of China. Hong Kong is a small, developed colony that has been run by the United Kingdom since 1841. Hong Kong has a higher standard of living and a different government than China. When Hong Kong joins China, it should be able to keep its free-market economy for many years. But no one knows for sure what will happen to Hong Kong after 1997.

▲ Hong Kong will become a part of China in 1997.

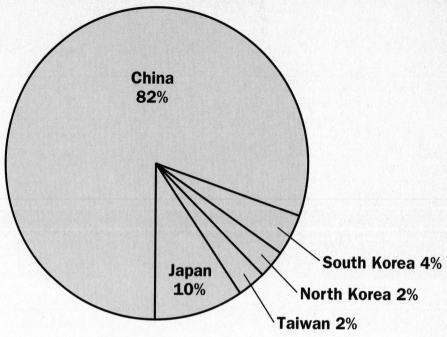

The third problem is protecting the **environment**. People in parts of this region are doing things that are hurting the land, plants, animals, water, and air. In China, the huge population causes problems for the environment. There is not enough land and water for all of these people to live. But China's population keeps growing by about 15 million people a year. In Japan, the environment has been hurt by air and water pollution from industries and cars.

People in many Pacific nations worry that nuclear weapons will hurt the environment. Nations from all over the world test nuclear weapons in this region. Pacific nations want their region to be a Nuclear Free Zone. In a Nuclear Free Zone, no nuclear weapons can be tested or even carried on ships and planes.

All of these nations face a fourth problem as they try to develop their economies. As these nations become modern, they may destroy or forget their traditions. In Australia, many Aborigines died when the British moved in. The British took over Australia's hunting land and brought deadly diseases. As the Aborigines changed to

◀ The ancient ways of life in Asia are changing.

fit in with the British laws and way of life, they gave up some of their interesting culture.

China also has an ancient culture that is changing as the nation becomes more modern. For more than 2000 years, most Chinese were **Confucians** who followed the teachings of Confucius. Today, millions of Chinese are Confucians. Confucians believe that the history of each person's family is very important. Confucians also think that people should do what their rulers tell them to do. For many years, Chinese schools taught Confucian ideas. When the Communists took over China, they tried to stop people from being Confucian.

The people of East Asia and the Pacific now have more food, more industries, and more schools than ever before. The region still has important problems that must be solved. But the people of this region are working hard to give their children a better future.

Using What You Learned

▼ **Think and Apply —— Analogies**

Use a word in dark print to finish each sentence.

**rice   command economy   developing nations   wool
Tokyo   overpopulation   North Korea**

1. Non-Communists are to South Korea as Communists are

    to _____.

2. Australia is to not enough people as China is to _____.

3. Japan is to cars as Australia is to _____.

4. A free market economy is to Taiwan as a _____ is to China.

5. Beijing is to China as _____ is to Japan.

6. Wheat is to Northern China as _____ is to Southern China.

7. New Zealand is to developed nations as the small Pacific islands are

    to _____.

▼ **Read and Remember —— Write the Answer**

Write an answer for each question.

1. Why is it dangerous for people in China to live near the Huang He

    River?_____

2. What is one natural disaster that happens in Japan? _____

    _____

3. What is one thing Japan is doing to keep the natural disasters from

    causing damage? _____

    _____

4. What happened to Korea in 1948? _____

_____

5. Why is the growing population hurting the environment in China?

_____

6. What will happen to Hong Kong in 1997? _____

_____

▼ Skill Builder —— Reviewing Pie Graphs

A pie graph is a circle that has been divided into parts. All the parts form a whole circle. Look at the pie graph on page 160. East Asia has five independent nations. The graph shows how the **total** population is divided among those five nations.

Use an answer in dark print to finish each sentence.

South Korea   82%   more   2%   Japan

1. _____ has 10% of East Asia's population.

2. Taiwan and North Korea each have _____ of the region's population.

3. China has _____ of all the people in this region.

4. The population of _____ is larger than that of Taiwan's but smaller than that of Japan's.

5. From the graph we can see that China has _____ people than the four other nations together.

Real Estate in Japan

The young Japanese couple is excited about their new weekend home. It is a small log cabin that costs $200,000. It is a five-hour drive from Tokyo, so weekends spent there are short. But the couple could not afford to buy land closer to the city. Even far from the city, the piece of land costs a lot of money.

In the city, land prices are so high that it can take up to seven years' pay to buy a small apartment. And that apartment is an hour by train from downtown Tokyo.

The reason for the high prices is simple. There are many people ready to buy, but there is very little land for sale.

TOKYO

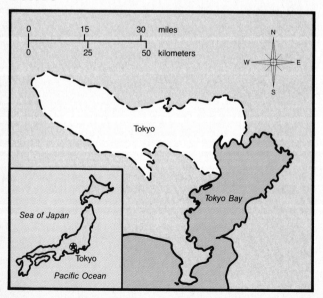

Location/Place

Tokyo is near the center of Honshu, Japan's largest island. The city is located on one of the few large flat areas in the whole country.

The city is the center of government and business in Japan. One out of every three Japanese lives within 100 miles of the center of Tokyo. The area is one of the most populated parts of the world.

Because there are so many people and so little land, prices for homes and land are very high. It costs twice as much to buy a home in Tokyo as it does to buy a home in New York City.

Human/Environment Interaction

Tax laws in Tokyo help cause the high price of real estate. Farmland is taxed very little. Many people plant crops but don't pick them so they can pay the lower tax on farmland. If all this land in Tokyo were used for building, the amount of space for houses would be doubled.

Many people in the government want to keep land prices high. The land brings in more taxes. But the farmers want to keep the taxes on their land low.

Movement

High land prices in Japan affect other parts of the world. Homes cost so much that Japanese have less money to spend on other things, including goods made in other countries.

The Japanese need for land is so strong that some Japanese turned to buying land and buildings in other countries rather than in Japan. Many Japanese bought buildings in the United States. One man bought nearly 200 homes in Hawaii and built 600 more in California. But by 1992, there was a big change. Prices for land in Japan fell. How do you think this may change ways of living in Japan?

▲ Japan's cities are crowded and expensive.

Write About It

Write a paragraph explaining to a person from Japan why he or she should buy land in the United States.

_____

_____

_____

_____

_____

_____

_____

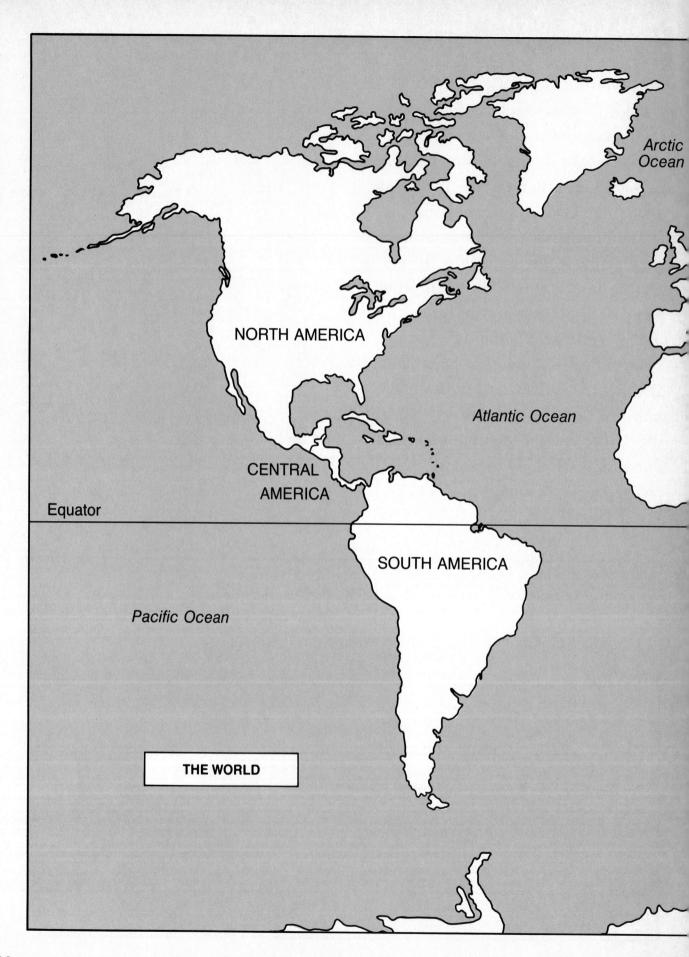

Arctic Ocean

NORTH AMERICA

Atlantic Ocean

CENTRAL AMERICA

Equator

SOUTH AMERICA

Pacific Ocean

THE WORLD

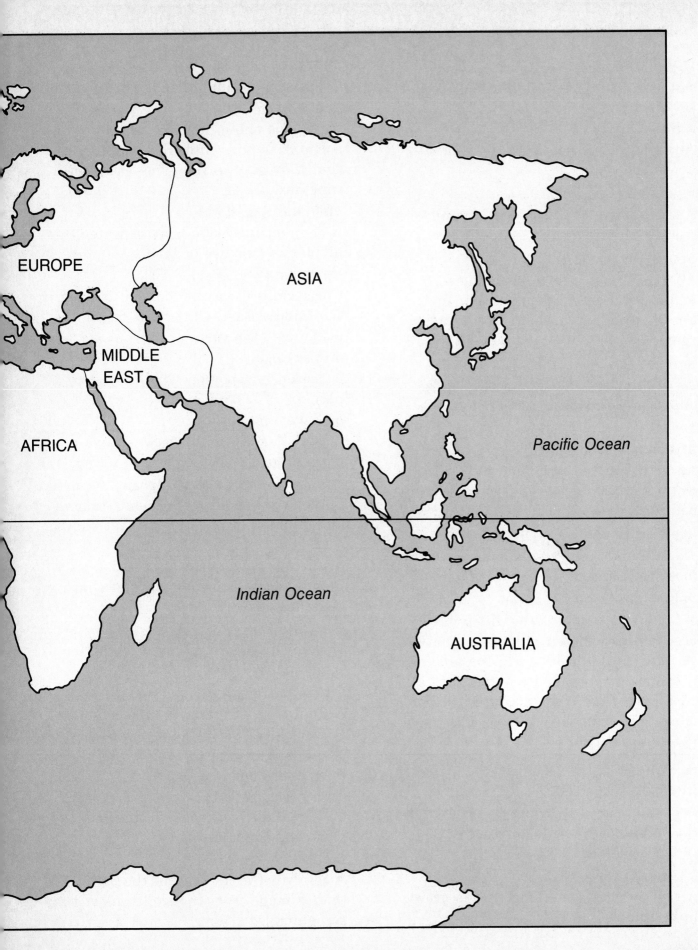

EUROPE

ASIA

MIDDLE
EAST

AFRICA

Pacific Ocean

Indian Ocean

AUSTRALIA

Glossary

agriculture page 65
Agriculture means farming and raising cattle.

altitude page 65
Altitude means how high an area is above the sea.

ancestors page 96
Ancestors are the people in a family who lived long ago.

apartheid page 70
Apartheid is a way to keep blacks, whites, and other groups apart. In South Africa, apartheid gives whites control of the nation.

archipelago page 111
An archipelago is a group of islands. Japan and Indonesia are archipelago nations.

artesian well page 153
An artesian well is a deep well with water that comes above ground without being pumped.

average income page 37
Average income is the amount of money most people earn in a year.

balance of trade page 146
A balance of trade is the difference between the amount of money a nation earns from its exports and the amount it spends on its imports. Japan has a good balance of trade because it exports more than it imports.

basin page 49
A basin is a low area of land.

Buddhist page 106
A Buddhist is a person who believes in the teachings of a religious leader called Buddha.

cash crop page 51
A cash crop is something that is grown to be sold.

cassava page 65
Cassava is a plant that is used for food.

caste page 100
A caste is one of four major groups that a Hindu is born into. Hindus believe that they stay in the same caste until they die.

channel page 17
A channel is a wide body of water that divides two bodies of land.

Christianity page 11
Christianity is a religion that started in the Middle East. Christians follow the teachings of Jesus.

citizen page 40
A citizen is a person who belongs to a nation.

civil war page 41
A civil war is a fight between two or more groups of people in one nation.

commercial agriculture page 92
Commercial agriculture means raising animals and growing crops that can be sold.

communication page 113
Communication means ways of sharing facts and ideas.

compete page 154
To compete means to try to do better than someone else.

Confucian page 161
A Confucian is a person who follows the teachings of the Chinese teacher Confucius.

consumer goods page 58
Consumer goods are things that people buy for their own needs. Cars and radios are consumer goods.

coral reef page 130
A coral reef is an area in the ocean that is made from the skeletons of tiny sea animals.

cottage industry page 93
A cottage industry is a business where people make goods in their own homes.

crossroads page 9
A crossroads is an area that people travel through to get somewhere else. The Middle East is a crossroads between Europe and Asia.

crude oil page 32
Crude oil is oil as it comes out of the ground.

dam page 18
A dam is a wall built to hold back the flow of a river.

defeat page 27
To defeat means to beat an enemy.

deforestation page 119
Deforestation means that the forests of a region are being destroyed.

delta page 16
A delta is land that is shaped like a triangle. It is formed when soil is left by a river flowing into the sea.

desertification page 79
Desertification means that grasslands get smaller and deserts grow larger.

dike page 158
A dike is a wall built to stop water from flooding the land.

disease page 20
A disease is a type of sickness.

distill page 39
To distill means to take out the salt from water. Kuwait distills sea water to make drinking water.

drought page 50
A drought is a long time with little or no rain.

earthquake page 132
An earthquake is the shaking and cracking of Earth's surface.

education page 80
An education is learning that people can get in schools.

electronic page 93
An electronic good is a machine that needs electricity in order to work. Computers are electronic goods.

environment page 160
The environment is the land, water, and air of a region.

erosion page 19
Erosion means that land is washed away by water or blown away by wind.

erupt page 112
To erupt means to burst out.

escarpment page 71
An escarpment is a sharp cliff along the edge of high, flat land.

expert page 81
An expert is a person who knows how to do something very well.

famine page 79
A famine is when many people die because there is not enough food.

Fertile Crescent page 32
The Fertile Crescent is the fertile region between the Tigris and Euphrates rivers.

foreign page 51
A foreign nation is any nation other than one's own nation.

foreign aid page 81
Foreign aid is money and help that one nation gives to another nation.

Hinduism page 100
Hinduism is the religion followed by most people in India. It teaches that souls are born again after people die.

holy page 24
A holy place or thing is special to one or more religions.

homeland page 26
A homeland is a nation that is a person's home. The Jews believe that Israel is the homeland promised to their people by God.

homelands page 73
Homelands are small, separate states in South Africa where many black South Africans are made to live.

human labor page 117
Human labor is work done by people. Most farmers in South and Southeast Asia use human labor instead of modern farm machines.

hunger page 78
Hunger is the pain people feel when they do not have enough to eat.

hydroelectric power page 19
Hydroelectric power is electricity that is made from the power of moving water.

illiterate page 80
An illiterate person does not know how to read or write.

international page 27
An international group is made up of at least two nations.

invest page 106
To invest means to put money into a business.

Islam page 11
Islam is a religion that began in the Middle East. It was started by a leader named Mohammed. Most people in the Middle East and North Africa follow Islam.

Jew page 11
A Jew is a person who follows Judaism. Jews were the first people to pray to one god.

Judaism page 11
Judaism is a religion that began in the Middle East.

kibbutz page 25
All people on a kibbutz share the work and tools, and the money earned from farming or other businesses.

kimono page 147
A kimono is a long robe that is worn by some people in Japan.

lava page 112
Lava is hot melted rocks from a volcano.

livestock page 153
Livestock are farm animals such as sheep, cows, goats, and pigs.

mainland page 129
A mainland is the part of a country or region that is on a continent. The islands of Japan are near the Asian mainland.

monsoon page 90
A monsoon is a wind that blows in one direction in the summer, bringing heat and heavy rains. A monsoon blows in a different direction in the winter, bringing cold, dry air.

mouth page 16
A mouth is where a river empties into a larger body of water. The mouth of the Nile River is on the Mediterranean Sea.

Muslim page 11
A Muslim is a person who believes in the religion of Islam.

natural disaster page 132
A natural disaster is something dangerous that is caused by nature. Volcanoes and floods are natural disasters.

nomad page 12
A nomad is a person who moves from place to place to find food.

nuclear energy page 146
Nuclear energy is used to make electricity.

nuclear weapon page 153
A nuclear weapon is a dangerous weapon that gets its power from nuclear energy.

oasis page 8
An oasis is a place in a desert that has water.

oil refinery page 32
An oil refinery is where oil is cleaned so that it can be used.

oil tanker page 30
An oil tanker is a ship that carries oil.

outback page 153
The outback is the dry inner region of Australia.

overpopulation page 119
Overpopulation means there are too many people in a region, and there is not enough food or work for everyone.

peace treaty page 40
A peace treaty is an agreement between two or more nations not to fight. Egypt and Israel signed a peace treaty in 1979.

percent page 26
Percent means the number of parts out of one hundred. When 83 percent of Israelis are Jews, this means that 83 out of every 100 Israelis are Jews.

petrochemical page 33
A petrochemical is something taken from oil after it comes out of the ground. Petrochemicals are used to make paint, medicines, and other goods.

plantation page 51
A plantation is a very large farm where one kind of crop is grown.

poverty page 37
Poverty means being poor.

priest page 100
A priest is a religious leader. There are Catholic, Hindu, and Buddhist priests.

production contract page 139
A production contract is an agreement between a farmer and the government. It tells how many crops a farmer must grow for the government.

protest page 140
A protest is when a person or group speaks out against the government.

pyramid page 17
A pyramid is a large stone building. It has four sides in the shape of triangles that meet in a point at the top.

racial group page 72
A racial group is made up of people who look more like each other than do people of other groups.

refugee page 40
A refugee is a person who leaves his or her own nation to find a safe place in a different country. Many refugees leave their homes during a war.

reservation page 152
A reservation is land set aside by the government for Aborigines or other people who have been moved from their homes.

sand dune page 8
A sand dune is a hill of sand formed by blowing wind.

savanna page 49
A savanna is a warm region that is covered with grassland.

sea level page 24
Sea level is the height of the sea or ocean.

seasonal wind page 90
A seasonal wind blows in one direction in the summer and in a different direction in the winter. A monsoon is a seasonal wind.

silt page 18
Silt is fertile, wet soil brought to the land when a river floods.

sisal page 65
Sisal is a plant that is used to make rope.

slash-and-burn agriculture page 91
Slash and burn agriculture means that farmers cut down trees, burn them, and then plant crops on that land. When the soil is no longer fertile, farmers move to another area and do the same thing again.

strait page 30
A strait is a narrow body of water between two larger bodies of water.

subsistence farmer page 52
A subsistence farmer grows only enough food for the farmer's family.

suburb page 70
A suburb is an area near a city that has homes and businesses.

swamp page 57
A swamp is an area of wet, soft land.

teak page 105
Teak is a tree found in Asia. Many people in Thailand cut down teak trees and sell the wood.

temple page 107
A temple is a building where people pray.

terrace page 92
A terrace is a large step that is built into a hillside. In Asia, terraces are used as fields for growing rice.

tourism page 66
Tourism is the business that helps people enjoy their visit to a region.

trade partner page 58
A trade partner is a nation that another country trades with.

tremor page 158
A tremor is a shaking movement made by an earthquake.

typhoon page 132
A typhoon is a dangerous tropical storm with very strong winds.

United Nations page 27
The United Nations is a group of nations from around the world that works for peace.

uranium page 153
Uranium is a mineral that is used for nuclear energy.

volcanic ash page 112
Volcanic ash is thick dust that comes out of a volcano.

wet rice farming page 91
Wet rice farming is how farmers grow rice in fields full of water.

wildlife page 48
Wildlife means the animals and birds of a region.

Index

List of Maps